O Taste and See

A FAMILY DEVOTIONAL GUIDE

Steve Baker

Foreward by Dr. Kathy Koch
Author of *8 Great Smarts*

All scripture quotations are taken from the English Standard Version Bible.

Steve Baker
318 Rio Hondo
Pipe Creek, Texas 78063
sandjbaker@gmail.com

Book Layout: Joyce Baker, published at SnowfallPress.com
Editors: Jonathan Bell and Cindy Martin
Contributors: T R Baker and Joyce Baker
Ordering Information:
Quantity sales. Special discounts are available on quantity purchases by corporations, associations, and others. For details, please email sandjbaker@gmail.com.

O Taste and See/ Steve Baker. —1st ed.

Acknowledgements

Allow me to first thank my Heavenly Father, the Lord Jesus for eternal life, and my walk with the Holy Spirit, which led to these devotions.

Thank you to Dr. Kathy Koch for the opportunity and permission to use her 'Five Core Needs' in the development of these devotional lessons. Her purposeful push gave the necessary motivation to put years of thoughts and insights to paper.

Thank you to each of my children for providing input and encouragement. T R Baker provided many of the stories and assisted in the writing of several devotions. Andrew, Katherine, Kevin, and Jon added insightful suggestions and editing. My wife, Joyce, has been the greatest encouragement and support. Your love was the central ingredient that enriched and nourished our family.

Thank you to many friends who helped proofread and provided support.

Foreward

Each of us is uniquely created in many beautiful ways. We know this from truths recorded in God's holy Word (e.g., Psalm 139:13-14 and Ephesians 2:10) and from raising children. Even "identical" twins aren't identical much less spouses and their children. We all have some things in common, though. For example, we're all created in God's image (Genesis 1:27), lost in need of a Savior (Romans 6:23), and strengthened through God's Word (Psalm 119:28). Also, each person is created by God with five core needs. They're not wants - they're needs. They're so necessary that they must be met. That's why God created them in each of us - so we can achieve the purpose for which we're born - to know Him personally. The needs drive us toward God. What are they?

Security: Who can I trust?

Identity: Who am I?

Belonging: Who wants me?

Purpose: Why am I alive?

Competence: What do I do well?

Many adults and children try to meet these legitimate needs in unhealthy, counterfeit, and temporary things. This doesn't work, so they keep searching. They're never settled. They're in bondage to the culture of popularity, money, position, power, and more. Contentment eludes them. Even the best things will fail us. This is also true of people. We're flawed and no one on earth can permanently and authentically meet our needs. We need God.

God meets our needs through His wisdom, love, presence, passion, care, power, concern, strength, answers, grace, mercy, call, faithfulness, truth, commitment, sacrifice, gifts... I could go on and on! But, I don't have to. Here, in these unique devotionals, Steve Baker shows you why and how God meets your needs. He addresses serious topics in relevant ways. Steve uses heroes from both the Old Testament and New Testament to share transforming truths. Illustrations and thought-provoking ideas serve to personalize the lessons so your children will embrace what you share with them. You'll benefit and so will they.

It's a delight to know Steve and Joyce Baker and their children. Steve and Joyce are some of my favorite people to be with and to think with. They heard me teach about the core needs and ran with them. They devoured my book about them (*Finding Authentic Hope and Wholeness: Five Questions That Will Change Your Life*), wrote a complete VBS program based on them, teach with them in mind, and now Steve wrote this for you. As you read these devotionals, I want you to think about what *you* are going to do with them. How will you take the truths here to heart? How will you know if you've been changed and if your teaching influenced your children? I know Steve wants these to affect you. So do I. Ask God to do a work in your life and for your children. Then watch. He will be faithful.

Dr. Kathy Koch, PhD
Author of *8 Great Smarts* and featured Focus on the Family speaker

Contents

O Taste and See – Getting Started

Using the Devotional Guides --

There are 52 devotional guides in this book, which coincides with the number of weeks in a year. My goal was to provide enough thought provoking material so that you can use each devotional for an entire week of discussion and activity. One day you can introduce the character trait topic with its definition and scriptural thought. The next day you can read the scripture text. Day three can be the reading of the devotional story. Day four through six can be for the "Taste Test" application and the "Scraping the Plate" discussions. I feel it is always best to let day seven be for rest and review.

There are eighteen character traits divided into five categories according to the core needs listed in Dr. Kathy Koch's forward and in her book "Finding Authentic Hope and Wholeness." Each of these essential human conditions can only be met through a genuine relationship with Jesus Christ. It is my hope that this book provides your family with great opportunities to grow closer to God and each other. I hope it strengthens the character of your family through Biblical truth.

Understanding the Devotional Guides --

In the Baker household, the times we gathered for meals, holidays, and Sundays were special in building our relationships. These times were opportunities to teach and develop quality character. The home is the greatest place to demonstrate Christianity and practice the growth in character. It should be a secure place to fail, be forgiven, and be renewed. Beginning in the home individuals can understand the connection between who they are and how that affects what they do. It is also the best place to begin the relationship of knowing God through Jesus Christ and the new identity He gives us, which molds our character.

Five family recipes, which stood the taste-test of time, became favorites in our home. These are comfort food meals and delicious dishes. In our family they represent the "Aahhhh...." that comes from being satisfied. That is why I have identified each of them with one of the five core needs. The devotionals are grouped according to the core needs, representing spiritual nourishment - and just for fun.

Security - Fried Chicken & Creamy Mashed Potatoes

Nothing makes one feel satisfied like a hearty and savory meal. Joyce's fried chicken is always moist on the inside with a crunchy crust. Her mashed potatoes are creamy and buttery with a perfect seasoning of salt and pepper. This was a meal every family member loved and rallied around, therefore we felt close, comfortable, and secure.

Identity - Nanny's Chocolate Pie

Nanny's chocolate pie recipe has been passed down through generations and Joyce inherited it from her mom, so don't even ask! It is rich and thick and truly deserves the title larrapin. There is no instant pudding here. This pie has become a trademark at holidays and special events. It is an identifiable dish to the Baker family.

Belonging - Sunday Pot Roast with Potatoes and Carrots

Sunday in a pastor's home meant early arrival at church and long Sunday mornings. So Sunday lunch had to be well thought out and prepared. Seasoned Pot Roast in the roasting pan or crock-pot became a common and easy fix, yet it was savory and filling. Rich dark au jus made into rich brown gravy was the perfect complement to the soft potatoes and sweet browned carrots. All these ingredients fit as if they were divinely designed to belong together. This meal was common and it set the stage for many a family time. Whether we were watching a football game together after church or relaxing at the table rehearsing God's goodness, we were reminded that this was where we belonged - together.

Purpose - Biscuits and White Gravy with Bacon

Yes, this is a Southern thing, but nothing says 'get-up-and-go' in the morning like a hearty breakfast. When we had a busy day ahead; the kids had a test or game going on, this was one of our go to recipes. It was quick and easy to fix. Because we served this on days of significant activity, biscuits and gravy became synonymous with purpose. Bacon never is a bad idea either.

Competence - Pancakes

No, not just plain ole' flapjacks like you see on the cover of the box. We liked to pour the pancake batter out to form shapes and patterns: race cars, animals, snowmen, and Christmas trees, even a Nativity. Pancakes like these became a family tradition for special times of getting together like holidays and birthdays. It took a lot of creativity to make each pancake so it has always been a reminder of the creative spirit within our family.

CHAPTER 1

Security

- Awareness
- Contentment
- Determination
- Love
- Endurance
- Hospitality
- Joyfulness
- Loyalty
- Humility
- Patience

AWARENESS - knowing and recognizing that something exists; finding wonder in and noticing the world around you

"Besides this you know the time, that the hour has come for you to wake from sleep. For salvation is nearer to us now than when we first believed." Romans 13:11

Scripture Text: John 4:1-42

Have you ever struggled looking for something? Maybe you lost your keys or wallet. You searched all over the house, thinking of anywhere you may have left it, only to realize it was right under your nose in plain sight. Many people are that way in their relationship with God. God has chosen that we must know Him through faith because any other way would distort the beauty and genuineness of such a unique, love relationship. If God were actually physically present and visible, everyone would believe in Him, but they might not love Him. They might not choose to willingly follow Him. As a matter of fact most people would not love Him; they would want to manipulate their relationship with God to get whatever they wanted out Him. They would treat God as the proverbial 'genie-in-a-lamp' or 'Santa Claus.' So God has chosen that *"the just shall live by faith."*

Many individuals have simply decided that since they cannot 'see' God, they won't believe in Him. This reminds me of the person who continues to go buy more resources at the store because they are unwilling to look around their house to find the supplies. They end up wasting their money and time, unaware that they had what they needed all along.

God, however, has made Himself known to us if we will just become aware. His creation speaks of His existence and design. *"The heavens declare the glory of God,"* the psalmist proclaimed. From the majestic mountains and grand oceans we see the power and strength of God. From the intricate design of bird feathers and butterfly wings to the consistency of the water cycle, we see God's genius. The similarity of design speaks to a single Creator.

Jesus met a woman at Jacob's well in Sychar who struggled in her faith. She believed in God, but did not know Him personally. She was the type that searched for someone to fill the void in her life instead of God. Yet she never found satisfaction or joy in other relationships; rather she just bounced from one relationship to another. As Jesus sat with her telling her about the eternal life she could have by faith in God, she was unaware that He was the Son of God and source of her fulfillment. Jesus expressed to her that God could be known spiritually if she would only believe. When Jesus revealed that He knew the longing of her heart and multiple relationships in which she had been involved unsuccessfully, she suddenly became aware that He was the Messiah, the 'Sent-One' from God. It was as if she woke from her sleep and could see clearly. What she had been searching for her whole life was right in front of her. God was only waiting for her to trust in Him by faith. Are you aware that God is waiting to have a relationship with you and satisfy your heart?

Taste Test:

Make a list of the many aspects of God's creation that reveal to you His existence. Visit a zoo, arboretum, or farm and explore the wonder of God's handiwork first hand. Read a book on God's creation evidences as a family like, *Not a Chance* by R. C. Sproul or numerous other books that can found online or in stores.

Scraping the Plate:

Read John chapters 3 and 4.

- *In chapter 3 there is a man steeped in religion but did not know God personally. How was he unaware of God even though he knew the scripture? How was he different and how was he similar to the woman in John 4? They were both unaware of their need to trust God by faith through Jesus Christ.*
- *Discuss whether each one in your family is truly aware of their need to trust Jesus as their Savior.*

Country Fried Chicken and Mashed Potatoes:

Knowing God personally and being aware of His presence with us provides great security. The fact that God wants to have a relationship with us and has gone out of His way to make Himself known to us, like Jesus did with the woman of Sychar, instills the confidence we need to approach Him.

CONTENTMENT - the state of being happy regardless of situations and satisfied; having no need of more
"But if we have food and clothing, with these we will be content." 1 Timothy 6:8

Scripture Text: Joshua 7

Scripture tells us, *"For God alone, O my soul, wait in silence, for my hope is from Him,"* Psalm 62:5. We are encouraged to look to God for our expectations and desires to be fulfilled. God made us with needs and wants. We all want to feel loved and appreciated. We need encouragement and help at times. When we look to other things or people to satisfy these needs, we leave God out of our life. This causes a discomfort, confusion, and sometimes disaster. God has a plan for our growth and maturity. If we truly trust Him, we must be content that His plan and the provision that He gives along the way are correct.

Joshua 7 tells the story of a man who doubted God's provision and took matters into his own hands. He was not content to wait on God's plan. The man's name is Achan and his discontentment was costly.

God's plan was simple: Trust Me and honor Me first and I will provide for you and protect you. Forty years before this story took place God had delivered His people, Israel, from Egypt. Achan and his family followed Moses, and then Joshua through the wilderness until God was ready to bring them into the land He had promised them. God's people had seen God's mighty hand of protection and provision many times.

God provided food in the desert, water from a rock, and protection from enemies. Now the people entered the land and won the first battle over the great city of Jericho. After having seen all these events, you would think that Achan would have no doubt that God was worth trusting.

God commanded the people that all the spoils (valuables) from the battle of Jericho were to be considered holy. Everything was to be gathered as an offering to give to the Lord from this first battle. The spoils from later battles would be theirs. Trust and honor God first was a commandment that Achan struggled with that time.

After the battle at Jericho, Achan discovered a bar of gold, some beautiful pieces of silver, and a lovely garment. He knew that he should turn them in to the offering, but he could not wait for future spoils. Rather than honor God's command, he kept those items for himself. Maybe he did not believe that God would give him what he wanted and needed in the battles to come. He decided not to trust God or honor God's command. He had to have what he wanted now. He could not be content to wait.

Because of his disobedience and discontentment, God withdrew His protection from the people of Israel until they repented. In the next battle, they fought against the small village of Ai. The Israelites were defeated and many men lost their lives. God held Achan responsible for this. God led Joshua to bring judgment upon Achan and his family. Their sin cost the lives of innocent soldiers, so God had Achan and his family put to death.

God has promised to supply our every need. He has a plan for that provision, but He requires us to honor Him first. *"Keep your life free from the love of money; and be content with what you have: for He has said, I will never leave you, nor forsake you,"* Hebrews 13:5.

Taste Test:

How hard is it for you to wait? Are you a child and can hardly wait until you are a teen? Or maybe as a teen, you can't wait until you are old enough to be considered an adult with its privileges? Discontentment robs us of the moment.

- Make a list of 'wants' that you have for the future when you get to the next 'stage' in life. (a car to drive, a girl/boy friend, a secure job, college, a certain income) Interview an older Christian who has gone through many stages of life.
- Ask if they experienced any dangers or blessings by waiting or not waiting on God.
- Ask if they trusted God for their provision in areas where you have listed your wants.
- How did it work out for them?

Scraping the Plate:

- Read 1 Timothy 6:7-10. Allow the idea of verses 9- 10 to sink in.
- Discuss the reason some fell away from the faith and have experience many sorrows.

- Compare that with Paul's encouragement to Timothy in verses 17-19.

Country Fried Chicken and Mashed Potatoes:

We can trust that God has our best interest in mind and He has a plan to fulfill our needs. Contentment is a benefit of the security we possess as we walk in obedience to His commands.

DETERMINATION - the quality that makes you continue trying to do or achieve something that is difficult

"I gave my back to those who strike, and my cheeks to those who pull out the beard; I hid not my face from disgrace and spitting. But the Lord God helps me; therefore I have not been disgraced; therefore I have set my face like a flint, and I know that I shall not be put to shame." Isaiah 50:6-7

Scripture Text: Daniel 1:1-21

Approximately 600 years before Christ, during a time of political upheaval in a world controlled by the power of dominant kings, Daniel, his three friends Hananiah, Mishael, and Azariah, and many other young men were carried away as captives into a foreign land. Doomed to serve as slaves, Daniel and his three friends were given the opportunity to be taught and trained as advisors to the King of Babylon, Nebuchadnezzar. This training was very difficult.

The first difficulty they faced during the training was eating the food that was provided for them. They were ordered to eat foods that were not clean according to Jewish religious custom. Daniel and his friends were devoted Jews and they did not eat certain meats or foods considered unclean. The King's diet was full of these foreign delicacies.

Daniel refused to eat the King's food and requested special permission from the King's guard to eat only vegetables. He was determined to be obedient to his religion and please God. Reluctantly they were given permission to eat their diet of vegetables for 10 days, and at the end of that time they were judged. I am sure that during those 10 days they wondered what their outcome would be. If they failed would they be punished or put to death? Maybe some of the other slaves tried to talk them into eating the King's food.

These 4 young men weighed the cost of their choice to honor God against the consequences of displeasing Nebuchadnezzar. They were determined that pleasing God was the right way to go. In the end Daniel, Hananiah, Mishael, and Azariah all passed the test with flying colors. They were in better strength and health than all the other slaves who had eaten the King's food. God honored their determination to be true to Him.

Taste Test:

As Christians there are certain things we should be determined to do to please God. The Hebrews reminded their children of God's requirements in the Shema, Deut. 6:4-9, whenever they entered or left their homes. Make a list of these things that would be good to follow as you try to live for Jesus every day. Make a decorative plaque or poster of these things and post it somewhere as a reminder.

Scraping the Plate:

Read 1 Corinthians 2:1-5 and compare it to the passage in Isaiah 50:6-7. In the same way the Messiah, Jesus Christ, was determined to obey and honor God's plan to die on the cross, Paul was also determined to please God. He was determined to not present anything other than the gospel truth to those to whom he preached. His determination to please God caused him to fear and tremble.

- Why do you think Paul was so fearful?
- What was he afraid of? Compare his fear in verse 3 with their faith in verse 5.
- Do you think that he was in awe of his responsibility to present the truth in an accurate way so others would genuinely believe?

Country Fried Chicken and Mashed Potatoes:

Because God makes us secure by proving His provision, we can remain determined to serve and be faithful to Him regardless of our situation.

LOVE – strong affection for another arising out of kinship or personal ties

"I have been crucified with Christ: It is no longer I who live; But Christ who lives in me. And the life I now live in the flesh I live by faith in the Son of God, who loved me and gave himself for me." Galatians 2:20

Scripture Text: 1 Samuel 18:1-4

The giving of gifts has always been a mark of love. According to Gary Chapman in his *The Five Love Languages,* it is one of the ways in which people communicate or understand love. Jonathan, the son of King Saul must have been one who demonstrated his love through the giving of gifts. 1 Samuel 18:1-4 clearly states that his soul was knit with David's and he loved him. Jonathan expressed his love by giving to David: his robe, personal garments, his sword, bow, and belt. These gifts represented Jonathan's understanding of David's calling to be King and his acceptance and submission to that position. These gifts showed Jonathan's commitment to care, serve, and protect David. The truth of this commitment was played out in their relationship through the years to follow as seen in 1 Samuel 19:11-7, 20:4, 23:16-18. These gifts were both valuable and sentimental to David.

God too has given because of love, and what He has given as a gift is extremely valuable to all who will receive it. Paul exclaimed in 2 Corinthians 9:15, *"Thanks be to God for His unspeakable gift."* John 3:16 expresses that truth with the beautifully poetic phrase, *"For God so loved the world, He gave...."*

God's gift was expressed over time and unwrapped at just the perfect moment.

From the beginning of creation, God foretold He was sending the gift of salvation - a Savior, who would conquer the works of Satan, destroy the curse of sin, and bring eternal life, peace, and forgiveness to all who would believe. A Savior was promised as the 'seed of woman' in Genesis 3:15, as the blessing of Israel to Abraham in Genesis 12, as Job's ransom in Job 33:24, the Deliverer and Redeemer of Israel in Psalm 72, the foundational corner stone of Israel in Isaiah 28:16, the righteous Lord in Jeremiah 23:5-6, and the list goes on.

The gift was given when the time on earth was perfect in God's plan according to Galatians 4:4 and as a fulfillment of those previous prophecies. "*She will bear a son, and you shall call his name Jesus, for he will save his people from their sins. All this took place to fulfill what the Lord had spoken by the prophet: 'Behold, the virgin shall conceive and bear a son, and they shall call his name Immanuel'.*" Matthew 1:21-23. Jesus shared His Father's love and confessed he came to seek and to save that which was lost by giving Himself. Titus 2:14 declares, "*Who gave himself for us to redeem us from all lawlessness and to purify for himself a people for his own possession who are zealous for good works.*"

God's love has offered a gift of immeasurable value - redemption. He offers to take our sin away in exchange for Jesus' righteousness, giving us salvation. As John proclaimed in 1 John 3, "*O, What love the Father has bestowed on us that we should be called the sons of God!*"

Taste Test:

Giving is such an awesome way to express love. God loved us when we did not even know Him or love Him back. Romans 5:8 *"But God shows His love for us in that while we were still sinners, Christ died for us."* Choose someone you know who may not know Jesus. Put together a gift package that includes something they will really need and appreciate. Add to your gift an invitational card that invites them to join you for church, or a card that tells your personal testimony of how you came to know Jesus. Deliver this gift and let them know you love them.

Scraping the Plate:

Read Romans 3:21-26. If any in your family have never made the decision to trust Christ as their own personal Savior, now would be a perfect time to share this truth and discuss their need. Let the Holy Spirit guide their heart to their own decision. Then read Romans 5:1-11 and list all the blessings we have as the recipients of God's gift.

Country Fried Chicken and Mashed Potatoes:

The love of God is the single most amazing and incomprehensible feature of His character. How He could love mankind who is sinful and rebellious goes beyond our understanding, but not beyond our grasp. He makes Himself available and that great love gives us the security of knowing that we can trust Him and run into His arms of grace.

ENDURANCE - the ability to do something difficult for a long time, or put up with pain and suffering that continues for a period of time

"I press toward the mark for the prize of the high calling of God in Christ Jesus." Philippians 3:14

Scripture Text: Isaiah 50:5-7

Can you imagine how devastating a situation it would be if the Lord Jesus Christ had stopped along the way to Calvary and quit? What if after having been beaten and ridiculed by Roman soldiers, while carrying the heavy cross up the Via Dolorosa, Jesus called out to His Heavenly Father to end the torture and choose a different way to save mankind?

We would be eternally lost, for as scripture declares, *"there is none other name under heaven whereby we must be saved,"... "and there is no remission of sins without the shedding of blood."* Thank goodness as Isaiah describes in Isaiah 50, Jesus set His face as a flint and went through with God's plan to be our Savior. The author of Hebrews said it well when he stated in Hebrews 12:2 that Jesus is, *"the founder and perfecter of our faith, who for the joy that was set before Him endured the cross, despising the shame, and is seated at the right hand of the throne of God"*. Jesus endured. He stuck it out because He wanted to please His Father. He persisted because He loved us enough to want to redeem us back to a right relationship with our Creator. He kept on going because He counted it a joy to defeat Satan, destroy sin, and rescue mankind.

Jesus' endurance is a motivation for us when we face temptations, trials, and life challenges. I read an amazing story in a book titled *The Greatest Sports Stories Never Told* by Bruce Nash and Allan Zullo. The true story of Ron Necciai epitomizes endurance. Ron Necciai set the world record for the most strikeouts in a professional baseball game. The year was 1952 and Ron was a lanky 19-year-old playing minor league professional ball in Bristol, Tennessee. Ron had previously quit pitching because he hit a batter once and broke his ribs. Since then, Ron was nervous pitching and his stomach would tie up in knots. However, his manager convinced him to try and pitch again.

On May 13, 1952, Ron began pitching against the Welch Miners. After the first three innings he had struck out eight batters and gotten one batter to ground out to the shortstop. His stomach was hurting so badly that he asked the manager to start warming up a replacement pitcher. The manager replied, "You're doing fine just hang in there." Ron did. Despite his nervous stomach and growing anxiety caused by the roar of the crowd, he closed in on surpassing the previous record of 25 strikeouts in a 9-inning game. He struck out the next 19 batters with amazing accuracy. The only difficulty along the way took place in the 9th inning. The leadoff batter had two strikes and then popped up a foul ball behind the catcher. Rather than catch it for the out, the catcher dropped it on purpose just so Ron could continue striking out the side and go for the record. Ron finished that batter off on the very next pitch. He struck out the second batter. Then the third batter of the inning swung and missed on his third strike, but the catcher missed the ball and it rolled to the backstop. It was recorded as a strikeout for the pitcher, but not an out since the batter reached base on a passed ball error. Ron struck out the last batter causing him to have struck out four batters in the 9th inning. Ron's incredible performance is still listed as the most famous minor league record.

Whatever we may be facing in life, whether it is a difficult job performance, a game challenge, trials of suffering, or temptations from the world, we are enabled by God's Holy Spirit to endure if we simply seek the Lord. Paul meant that when he wrote to the Philippians. "*For His sake I have suffered the loss of all things and count them as rubbish, in order that I may gain Christ and be found in Him, not having a righteousness of my own that comes from the law, but that which come through faith in Christ, the righteousness from God that depends on faith - that I may know Him and the power of His resurrection, and may share His sufferings, becoming like Him in His death, that by any means possible I mat attain the resurrection from the dead.*" God longs to strengthen you and help you to endure that you might know Him more closely and that He might display His righteousness in you.

Taste Test:

Some board games seem to take forever. Some challenges require a lot of endurance.

Choose a suitable challenge for your family that would tax your current level of patience and endurance. Give it a try.

- Play that board game that takes half the night to finally get a winner, with everyone staying up to congratulate the champion.
- Run that 5K or 10K together.
- Tackle that garage-cleaning project.

Scraping the Plate:

Read Isaiah 50:5-7 and 53:3-12. Discuss how much Jesus endured as this passage prophetically described Jesus' death and suffering. Notice how, according to verse 10 of Isaiah 53, it was God's will to bring prosperity through Jesus' suffering. How have we benefitted or prospered because of Jesus' death? Would we have been blessed to have Him intercede for us if He had not endured?

Country Fried Chicken and Mashed Potatoes:

Knowing that Jesus was willing to endure all that He went through to accomplish our salvation, gives us the security of His love and the faithful fulfillment of that saving work.

HOSPITALITY - being generous and friendly in treatment of visitors; the activity of providing food and refreshment for people who are guests

"Though we speak in this way, yet in your case, beloved, we feel sure of better things - things that belong to salvation. For God is not unjust so as to overlook your work and the love that you have shown for His name in serving the saints, as you still do. And we desire each one of you to show the same earnestness to have the full assurance of hope until the end," Hebrews 6:9-11

Scripture Text: 2 Kings 4:8-37

Some people are only generous and hospitable in their giving or service because they hope to receive something in return. That was not the case of the lovely lady in the scripture text today. The woman, from the village of Shunem, is never named nor is her husband, yet she is honored with two chapters in God's Word. This woman chose to be generous and hospitable with what she had, not expecting anything in return. Her trust was in God alone.

The Shunemite lady's story begins with mystery about her past. She carried a dark secret of pain and loneliness. For a long time she had wanted children, but God had not blessed her with any. She did not tell anyone of this hidden longing. As the story progresses, we realize that she had actually given up hope of ever having a child. Her desire, she stated, was to simply be at peace and contentment among her own people. Instead she gave herself to the care of others with what she did possess. She possessed the ability to bake and serve.

One day, as the prophet Elisha passed by, she invited him in for bread. We know that she was not being gracious with some hope of reward, because she did not even know who he was at first. When she did perceive that he was a prophet, she built a guest room on her rooftop so he would have a place to rest. This she did simply to honor him as a prophet of God. Elisha used her guest room as a place to rest when he traveled.

God saw this woman's precious heart and He did honor her hospitality because it came from a heart of genuine love. God gave her a son, raised that son back to life after an accident, guided her through a famine, and restored her lands back to her after the famine ended. Her hospitality is the type of character encouraged by genuine love. *"Love is kind..,"* 1 Corinthians 13:4. Genuine character is one thing God loves to honor and reward. You cannot seek the reward by putting on a 'front' of character, but when you truly seek to behave like the Father in heaven - He notices.

Taste Test:

The woman of Shunem encourages us to open our hearts and home. Plan to invite some friends or acquaintances over to your home for a meal. Listen to their story and ask them questions so that you can learn how to pray for them. Make the evening all about your guests.

Scraping the Plate:

Do a family inventory list together. Let each family member list the ways in which they feel like they are hospitable to others, including within the family. Use this as a teaching moment to evaluate the motive and intent of one's works. Discuss Hebrews 6:11 where we are encouraged to be diligent in hospitality. Could "*to the full assurance of hope unto the end,*" be a reminder that God is watching and keeping an account of our works?

Country Fried Chicken and Mashed Potatoes:

As we share our blessings and provision with those in need, we open ourselves up to risk. Being hospitable demonstrates how in our trust of God, we know we are secure in His grace.

JOYFULNESS - the feeling of great happiness or delight evoked by wellbeing, success, or good fortune

"Then he said to them, 'Go your way. Eat the fat and drink sweet wine and send portions to anyone who has nothing ready, for this day is holy to our Lord. And do not be grieved, for the joy of the Lord is your strength." Nehemiah 8:10

Scripture Text: John 15:9-11

Our Heavenly Father greatly desires for us to be full of joy. He wants us to spread the joyful news of eternal life through His Son Jesus Christ. Our mood can be and should be contagious. When one person is in a bad mood, it tends to bring others down with them. When someone yawns, it starts a chain reaction. In the same way joy and laughter are contagious.

Growing up in church I always enjoyed singing the hymn, *The Joy of the Lord is My Strength.* One verse repeats the words: *"He fills my mouth with laughter, I sing ha, ha, ha."* At the end of that verse we would repeat it, changing all the words to sounds of laughter. This would quickly turn into real laughter. The mood in the room would be light and joyous. There are very few things that lighten the spirit like laughter with good friends and family.

King Solomon wrote in Proverbs 17:22a, *"A joyful heart does good like a medicine."* Studies have shown this to be true. A joyful countenance is believed to lead to longer and healthier living. Although it is not always easy to be in a good mood, as sometimes we will face difficult times and experience depression, which can take a foothold. Jesus longed for us to be full of His joy. John15:9-11 states, "*As the Father has loved me, so have I loved you. Abide in my love. If you keep my commandments you will abide in my love, just as I have kept my Father's commandments and abide in His love. These things have I spoken to you, that my joy may be in you, and that your joy might be full.*"

Another reason to be full of joy is to overcome temptation. Galatians 5:22 tells that one of the fruit of the Spirit is joy. These fruit of the Spirit help us live a godly life. According to Nehemiah, Ezra read the book of the law to the Israelites then told them not to grieve or be upset, because the joy of the Lord was their strength. We therefore can have strength to overcome temptation and depression as we rejoice in God's provisions.

Taste Test:

Sing or listen to one of your favorite songs together. That will bring joy. There are many ways to lift the spirit. 1 Peter 1:8-9 tells us to rejoice for the eternal life we have been given in Jesus Christ. Other ways include: reading the book of Psalms, doing fun family activities together, singing joyous hymns.

Do you know anyone who needs the joy of the Lord in his or her life right now? Maybe they are struggling with being discouraged or with a particular temptation. Encourage them to confess their need to God and rejoice in His provision of forgiveness and care. As they rejoice by faith, even when they don't feel like it, the joy will come.

Scraping the Plate:

Why do you think people get discouraged or depressed? Why do people constantly try to find things or activities to make themselves happy? Do you think that they may not know the joy that comes as a by-product of knowing and having a relationship with God through Jesus Christ? Read Nehemiah 7:9-12 and discuss the difference between having joy in God as opposed to being happy with possessions or money.

Country Fried Chicken and Mashed Potatoes:

The joy of the Lord is a by-product of being in right relationship with Him. That relationship strengthens us and removes fear; we are joyfully secure in Christ.

LOYALTY - a feeling of strong support for someone or something

"Whoever pursues righteousness and kindness will find life, righteousness, and honor." Proverbs 21:21

Scripture Text: Ruth 2

There was once a young woman whose father was deathly ill and he was unable to care for himself. I met and knew this young woman when I worked as a chaplain ministering to the dying. She sacrificed a lot because she had dedicated herself to caring for her dying father. His care took all of her time and energy. What amazed me was the fact that he had abandoned her when she was young. For reasons I never heard, he had left the family years before. However, in her young adulthood, she reached out to him to rebuild a relationship. She was a strong Christian and he was not. She learned of his poor condition and invited him to move in with her. As her father's disease process worsened, her husband left her, but she continued to care for her dad. She had to quit her job, temporarily. Yet, in spite of the difficulties, she had the privilege of seeing her dad come to trust in Jesus before his death. This woman embodied a great example of loyalty.

The Bible tells a similar story in the book of Ruth. This short story is a dynamic capsule of the gospel. God reaches out to redeem the lost and hurting. But the character of Ruth is especially intriguing as she displays the kind of loyalty mentioned above. As the story goes, Naomi and her family moved away from Israel and into Moab because of a famine. While there,

Naomi's two sons married Moabite young women. One was named Orpah and the other was Ruth. Over a ten-year time span, Naomi's husband and both sons passed away, leaving all three women widows. Soon after, Naomi decided to return to Israel, but she was discouraged and she told her daughters-in-law to return to their own families. She was depressed and wanted to change her own name to a name that meant, "bitter." Naomi's life was full of pain and loneliness.

Orpah agreed and returned to her family there in Moab, however, Ruth makes one of the most beautiful statements in scripture. *"Do not urge me to leave you or to return from following you. For where you go I will go, and where you lodge I will lodge. Your people shall be my people, and your God my God. Where you die I will die, and there I will be buried."* Ruth 1:16-17. From that point on, Ruth pursues serving and being kind to Naomi. She returns to Israel and works as a beggar in the fields gleaning grain. She listens and obeys all of Naomi's instructions. Because of this act of complete loyalty, God blesses Ruth and raises up a kinsman to redeem her from her situation of loss and poverty. Boaz marries Ruth and buys back the property that once belonged to Naomi's family. All was restored.

Scripture says that a faithful man is hard to find in Proverbs 20:6. It refers to one who is loyal to others rather than just himself. Ruth was loyal in the manner God desires, and you can be too, as you allow His grace to lead you.

Taste Test:

Sometimes loyalty can be shown by the kind deeds we do to help each other, and sometimes it can be expressed by the kind words we say to them.

Just like Ruth promised her support and kindness to Naomi, why don't you write a note of encouragement telling of your love and support to someone in your family?

Hide it under their pillow so they can find it later.

Scraping the Plate:

Discuss the whole story of Ruth and how others were loyal as well: God, Naomi, and Boaz. Can you see how God's loyalty to mankind plays an important role in the redemptive plan?

Country Fried Chicken and Mashed Potatoes:

Believers need to know that they are secure in the support they have from each other, just like they should know God will never leave them or forsake them.

HUMILITY - the quality or state of mind where one does not think of himself as better than others; lowliness of heart; meekness of spirit

"Humble yourselves in the sight of the Lord, and He will lift you up." James 4:10

Scripture Text: John 12:1-8, Matthew 26 and 27:3-5

Sometimes scripture lays out a story that clearly demonstrates the difference in the character of two people. In John's text there is a stark difference between the hearts of Judas Iscariot and Mary, the sister of Lazarus and Martha. At a feast in the home of Simon the leper, Mary poured out a very expensive ointment on Jesus' feet to honor and anoint Him. This was done as an act of devotion to Jesus, and showed Mary's humility because it was servant's work to attend to the feet. Judas, however, took offense. He complained that the perfume could have been sold and much money given to the poor. But he was not really interested in the poor, as verse 6 points out. He was a thief at heart and wanted more for himself.

In the Matthew text, Judas devised an elaborate plan of deception. He went to the chief priests and offered to deliver Jesus to them if they would pay him. The chief priests had wanted to catch Jesus away from the crowds where they could arrest him secretly. Maybe Judas thought that after he collected his money from the chief priests and led them to Jesus, Jesus would fight back and escape again. He would be richer and no one would be the wiser to his scheme. His plan backfired when Jesus let himself be taken, tried, and crucified by the religious leaders. In horror and regret, Judas repented of his deed. He returned the dishonestly gained money and went out and hanged himself. He will forever be remembered as the traitor to Jesus for his prideful dishonesty and greed.

Mary, on the other hand, is remembered with great respect. Jesus said of her, *"Assuredly, I say to you, wherever this gospel is preached in the whole world, what this woman has done will also be told as a memorial to her,"* Matthew 26:13. Mary did not do it to gain honor; she did it to honor Christ. God fulfilled His word to lift her up because of her humility.

A sad but comical story can be found of baseball pitcher, Alva "Bobo" Holloman, who played briefly for the 1953 St. Louis Browns. Bobo was a 27-year-old rookie relief pitcher who thought he should be a starter. In his relief appearances he was not that impressive, sporting an ERA of 8.49. However, because of his continual pestering, his manager gave him a chance to start a game. Amazingly, he accomplished what no other pitcher had ever done in the major leagues until that time. He pitched a no-hitter his first appearance as a starter. The game was riddled with error and luck, but his no-hitter remained intact. Sadly, Bobo never proved to be the star that he boasted he was. The arrogant young baseball player finished the only year of his major league career with a 3-7 record and an ERA of 5.23. He stands as an example of Proverbs 29:23, *"One's pride will bring him low, but he who is lowly in spirit will obtain honor."*

Taste Test:

Competitive sports can be a great opportunity to learn humility. Sometimes a player needs a little 'fire-in-the-belly' attitude to play hard. For an athlete of any skill level the question is: How does one play with confidence and aggressiveness while maintaining humility?

- This can be taught as you play games. Plan regular family game nights. There will be some games that certain members of the family are better at than others. As you play, recognize and compliment good play. However, when this leads to possible boasting or the belittling of other players, stop the game. Remind each other that no one has the abilities they possess apart from the gifting of God. Since God made us unique individuals, everyone has worth and value; no one should be devalued for a seeming lack of skill. Just because some are better at one sport than others does not allow for boasting.
- Encourage those who are good at a sport to help and teach others. This builds teamwork and humility.

Scraping the Plate:

Read 1 Peter 5:5. Clothing is something we wear that others can see instead of our nakedness. How can we wear humility as a garment for others to see? What does humility as a garment cover that we do not want others to see? (Remember Judas and Bobo) How was Mary clothed in humility?

Country Fried Chicken and Mashed Potatoes:

When God's children understand that they are secure in their relationship with Him and nothing will ever separate them from His love, they do not need the affirmation of the world. We can remain humbly secure because our Father loves us and accepts us.

PATIENCE - the state of being able to remain calm and not annoyed when waiting for a long time; maintaining a inner peace when dealing with problems or difficult people

"*Wait for the Lord; be strong, and let your heart take courage; wait for the Lord.*" Psalm 27:14

Scripture Text: Acts 1-2

It can be hard to wait when you are looking forward to something exciting. I remember as a child how hard it was to wait day after day sitting in a school classroom in late spring, anticipating the freedom of summer. I longed for the warm, lazy days of leisure and the fun-filled days of playing baseball. My mind struggled to wait until there was no homework and lectures. Patience is a necessary quality that enables one to maintain the ability to accomplish tasks while looking forward to a desired goal. I struggled to focus on the goal of my schoolwork while I was daydreaming about summer.

There are some great examples of patience in the Bible. Job was patient as he waited for God to bring healing to his broken body. Joseph was patient while he waited for God's deliverance from the Egyptian prison. David was patient as he roamed the countryside, fleeing from King Saul, and waiting for God to establish him as the next king.

One of the best examples of patience is in Acts 1 and 2. Jesus had told his disciples to return to Jerusalem and wait. He had promised to send to them the Holy Spirit of God who would fill them with power. Can you imagine their anticipation?

They had walked with Jesus for three years and seen His mighty miracles. These men and women had then watched Christ crucified and, amazingly, rise from the dead. I imagine they were more anxious than I was as a schoolboy. What an exciting and unprecedented event!

From the time of Jesus's resurrection, he had appeared to them several times over a period of about 40 days. The comparison of John 20:19, 26 with Acts 1:12-24 provides an interesting contrast. Previously, they had been hiding in Jerusalem with no direction; now their hearts were filled with anticipation and hope. This hope encouraged them to plan for their service to the Lord in the future. They chose Matthias to take Judas's place as one of the twelve apostles. They also gathered together daily to pray and devoted themselves to the study of God's word.

Psalm 27 gives us that same encouragement to wait on the Lord with anticipation. God has great plans in which we are to serve Him daily. We are told to be faithful with the promise that God is our stronghold in life. As with the disciples in Acts 1-2, the Holy Spirit is promised to be with us for power and provision. The psalmist put it a different way, "*He will hide me in his shelter in the day of trouble; He will conceal me under the cover of His tent; He will lift me high upon a rock. And now my head shall be lifted up above my enemies all around me, and I will offer in His tent sacrifices with shouts of joy; I will sing and make melody to the Lord.*" Like the disciples in Acts were anticipating the coming Holy Spirit, we have the added joy of anticipating Jesus's return. Though we do not know the day or the hour, we are encouraged to wait for Him during our time of service. "*Therefore, my beloved brothers, be steadfast* (patient*), immoveable,* *always abounding in the work of the Lord, knowing that in the Lord your labor is not in vain,"* 1 Corinthians 15:58. Set your eyes on the goal and stay busy, summer is coming!

Taste Test:

One of the marks of getting discouraged in our work is 'fainting' the Bible says. *"And let us not grow weary in doing good, for in due season we will reap if we do not give up.* (faint)" Galatians 6:9. Sometimes our own cares also sidetrack us and we forget God's purposes.

- Make an inventory sheet with two columns.
- Label the left column "Past Work" and the right column "Today's Work."
- Under each column list the things you as a family are doing in service to the Lord.
- Have they increased or decreased?
- These may naturally change and even decrease as you get older, but compare the two columns and ask yourselves whether you are doing all you can and should in your service for the Lord today.

Scraping the Plate:

Read Revelation 22:12. Have you forgotten the joyous anticipation of His return when you will stand before Him, offering your talents as a gift? Would you be satisfied with how you have served if He came back today? Discuss ways you as a family can serve the Lord together, if you are not already. Examine whether your service is currently full of joy for the anticipation of His return and not out of a mundane sense of duty. Discuss how waiting patiently entails continuing to serve faithfully?

Country Fried Chicken and Mashed Potatoes:

The promises of God and their fulfillment throughout scripture give us the secure knowledge that He will fulfill the promises for which we are waiting: Heaven and glorious deliverance from this world, new bodies, and freedom from sin. We can patiently wait as we serve Him because His Word is true.

CHAPTER 2

Identity

- Availability
- Endurance
- Flexibility
- Honesty
- Humility
- Righteousness
- Contentment
- Love
- Responsibility
- Courage
- Kindness

AVAILABILITY - the quality or state of being ready and accessible to others or in a situation

"But in your hearts honor Christ the Lord as holy, always being prepared to make a defense to anyone who asks you for a reason for the hope that is in you; yet do it with gentleness and respect." 1 Peter 3:15

Scripture Text: 2 Timothy 4:2, 11-18

"But the Lord stood by me and strengthened me... " (vs. 17). Paul makes this bold, affirming statement of God's faithful availability to Timothy as he was awaiting execution. Paul was giving his defense before the courts and no one had come to support him. He was going through dark and lonely times and even lists some of those trials. *"Demas has forsaken me." "Crescens and Titus have departed." "Alexander the coppersmith did me much evil." "No man stood with me."*

Paul did not focus on these difficulties or pain, Instead he trusted that the God, who promised over and over again in scripture to be with us, would keep His word. Paul knew God had made that promise to His children beginning with Abraham and continuing through history. Like this statement in Jeremiah 42:11, *"Do not fear him, declares the Lord for I am with you, to save you and to deliver you from his hand."* That promise was passed on through Jesus to the disciples. *"Lo, I will be with you even to the end of the age."*

Paul wanted to encourage Timothy that even in trial or loss, God is always available to guide and help us. It is so amazing that the God of Creation, who holds the universe in place, would care to be available for our needs. Yet He says, *"Call to Me, and I will answer you, and will tell you great and hidden things that you have not known,"* Jeremiah 33:3. God's availability is one reason for our hope. Paul boldly concluded, *"The Lord shall deliver me from every evil work, and will preserve me to His heavenly kingdom." (vs 18).*

Knowing that God is a God of promise and fulfillment, we have great hope and should be available to His service. Paul encourages us to be *"instant in season and out of season,"* (2 Tim. 4:2) to preach the gospel. That was Peter's encouragement as well. We should be available to share our hope with anyone, at any time, " *always being prepared to make a defense to anyone who asks you for a reason for the hope that is in you."* 1 Peter 3:15

No matter what you may be going through, good times or difficult times, God is with you. Because He is with you, be available for His service. The brightest lights are those who shine through the darkness.

Taste Test:

Put the promise to test, today. Take time to get alone with Him and spend time reading His Word. He has promised to be with us, so ask Him to speak to you through the reading of God's Holy Word.

- As you read look for the acronym HOPE:
  - ✓ H stands for Him. Look for God himself.

- ✓ O stands for Obedience. Look for things God calls you to do.
- ✓ P stands for promise. Look for the promises of God.
- ✓ E stands for Error. Look for things about yourself that need to change. We all need to seek God's forgiveness of sin and grow in character from our weaknesses.

- Mark these in the margin of your Bible. God can use this simple tool as a way of speaking to you, and it will encourage you of His presence.

Scraping the Plate:

- Reading this devotion is a great time to review the things that God has done for your family in the past. Remembering God's faithfulness in your past experiences strengthens your trust in His continued presence, increasing your faith and hope.
- After you rehearse past experiences, share with each other the things you learned as you spent time alone with God in the past week. Now, address ways in which you can be prepared to share your faith and the hope that is in you, with others.

Nanny's Chocolate Pie:

God is available to those who are His; therefore, we should be available to God.

ENDURANCE - the ability to do something difficult for a long time, or put up with pain and suffering that continues for a period of time

"As an example of suffering and patience, brothers, take the prophets who spoke in the name of the Lord. Behold, we consider those blessed who remained steadfast. You have heard of the steadfastness of Job, and you have seen the purpose of the Lord, how the Lord is compassionate and merciful." James 5:10-11

Scripture Text: Psalm 60:1-5

The Psalmist explained in Psalm 60:1-5 an amazing truth that many believers want to ignore. *"O God, You have cast us off; you have broken us down; you have been displeased; O, restore us again! You have made the earth tremble; you have broken it; heal its breaches, for it is shaking. You have shown your people hard things; you have made us drink the wine of confusion. You have given a banner to those who fear You, that it may be displayed because of the truth, that you beloved may be delivered. Save with Your right hand and hear me..."*

The fact that God shows His own people "hard things" is a truth of life. Every one experiences difficult events and experiences. He even allows His children to experience these difficulties like exercises. They help us grow stronger in faith and character like the prophets of old which James describes in James 5:10-11.

Writer, Margaret Bottome, once told the story of receiving some beautiful pink flowers. When she inquired what they were, she was told they were 'rock flowers.' The giver explained that these delicate flowers grew among the mountain rocks where no soil could be seen. Margaret was so impressed by the thought that God's most precious flowers, His people, also grow best when raised through tough and desperately hard circumstances.

God may show a peculiar tenderness for His 'rock flowers' that He may not have for His tulips or roses. Truly God our Father has a tenderness for those of His children who seek to know Him and draw close to Him during the difficult times of pain, suffering, and sorrow. Those who endure suffering and difficulties in order to grow stronger may be more useful to the Lord in displaying His grace, because God reveals that tenderness to His 'rock flowers' through His presence and care. We would never know His healing power and deliverance if we did not experience sickness, weakness, or captivity.

The psalm continues stating, "*You have made us drink the wine of confusion...*" There are times when we simply do not understand and have to trust the Lord as He is directing our lives toward the growth and goodness that we need. These are times when we cannot feel or see the "soil" of His provision. We are reminded in Proverbs 3:5 not to lean on our own understanding but to trust in the Lord with all our heart. The psalmist goes on to relay God's goal, "That you may be delivered." God's work is always a work of redemption. Herein lies the tenderness of the Father's love; He longs to deliver us from the bondage of things in this life that keep us from the fullness of His eternal life in Christ Jesus. His tender workings, even through hard times, give us great reason to endure.

The Taste Test

One of the most difficult yet simplest exercises is called planking. It is an isometric core-strength exercise that involves holding a difficult horizontal position for an extended period of time. Therefore it is an exercise in endurance. Take turns trying to lie on your back and hold your feet six inches off the floor while keeping your legs straight. Then try lying on your stomach raising your body up onto your elbows and toes, again while keeping your whole body as straight as possible. Can you do these exercises for 30 seconds? 2 minutes? Or more.

Scraping the Plate:

Read James 5:10-11 and discuss the difficulties of Job and the prophets.

- What kept them going?
- What made them continue trusting the Lord?
- Are there areas in your life that you struggle to endure under? Maybe subjects at school or work, maybe relationships with certain people are stressful. Maybe goals you seek to achieve are tedious and keep you down.
- What do you think James meant when he encourages us to keep our eyes on the end?

Nanny's Chocolate Pie:

Know that you are the chosen of God and He promises His love and care. Because of your identity as God's "rock flowers" you can be sure of His care even when life is hard.

FLEXIBILITY - the state of being able to easily change or adjust; ability to do different things, adapt to new and different or challenging requirements

"For this is a gracious thing, when, mindful of God, one endures sorrows while suffering unjustly. For what credit is it if, when you sin and are beaten for it, you endure? But if when you do good and suffer for it you endure, this is a gracious thing in the sight of God. For to this you have been called, because Christ also suffered for you, leaving you an example, so that you might follow in His steps." 1 Peter 2:19-21

Scripture Text: Acts 16:6-12

When situations in life are a source of irritation, it may be because God is trying to move us in a different direction. God uses our circumstances to guide and direct us. It may be through suffering which He allows us to endure or through trials we face from others that God moves us to a place of constant service and worship in our journey with Him. Being flexible means being attentive and available to the teaching of the Holy Spirit.

This was true in Paul's life as he went on his missionary journey through Asia Minor. Paul desired to go one way toward Turkey, yet the Holy Spirit wanted Paul to go west and cross over into southern Europe. God gave Paul a vision of a man standing on the shore of Macedonia praying and calling out, "Come over into Macedonia and help us." This took great flexibility from the mission team to change their plans; an even a greater need for flexibility as they faced opposition.

In light of the vision, Paul made plans to sail to Macedonia. He and his team eventually arrived at Philippi. They had quick success in reaching a well-known and affluent woman named Lydia. She listened intently to their teachings and trusted the Lord Jesus as her Savior.

Their obedience was also met with suffering because they were followed about by a young demon possessed girl who was used by businessmen to tell the fortunes of people for a profit. Paul cast the demon out of the damsel and this ended the business practice of these local men. Outraged, they caught Paul and Silas, took them before the rulers, had them beaten, and thrown into prison.

Where was the blessing of being flexible to follow the Holy Spirit in all of this, one might ask? God always knows what He is doing. That night as Paul and Silas sang in prison, probably to the amazement of the other prisoners and the jailor, God shook the prison with an earthquake. The events that followed led to the jailor and his whole family's salvation and the church at Philippi was born. None of this would have happened if Paul and Silas had not been flexible to listen to the leading of God's Spirit, flexible to endure unjust suffering knowing that God was with them, and flexible to praise God in light of the irritations they endured.

Taste Test:

Take an elderly saint in your church out to lunch one day and visit with them about the character of flexibility.

- Ask them to tell you stories of when God moved them or changed the direction of their life.
- Was it hard?
- How did they respond?
- Was it worth it if they obeyed?
- Ask them to tell you the blessing of listening to the Spirit of God.

Scraping the Plate:

Discuss the scripture text in Acts 16:6-40.
Read the whole story.

What might have been different in history if Paul and Silas had gone the other way into Bithynia? Would we have ever heard the gospel or would we have ever heard of Paul? Would God have had to raise someone else up to spread the gospel to Europe? We can be extremely grateful for Paul's obedient flexibility.

Nanny's Chocolate Pie:

Our identity as God's children requires that we are growing in character and changing by putting on the Lord Jesus Christ. This requires our flexibility in allowing God to lead us.

HONESTY - the state of being and actions of being good and truthful; free from fraud or deception; not hiding the truth about someone or a situation; not being willing to deceive

"O Lord, who shall sojourn in your tent? Who shall dwell on your holy hill? He who walks blamelessly and does what is right and speaks truth in his heart;" Psalm 15:1-2

Scripture Text: Genesis 3

Many times it seems contrary to our nature to be honest, like the little child who sneaks into the kitchen and snatches a piece of their mom's chocolate pie before dinner. Even with the evidence of a chocolate 'mustache' as proof of her crime, she will deny it. Children may be afraid many times of suffering the consequences of doing wrong.

Lying is one of key characteristics of the devil. He is known as the father of lies in John 8:44. From the beginning in the Garden of Eden, the old devil, Satan, has used lying to deceive and trick people into falling into the traps of sin. As we read the story in Genesis 3, observe how Satan cleverly twisted the truth. In verse four he lied about death and he twisted the truth about their understanding to make Eve question God's compassion and motives. The consequence of their sin was death and separation from God.

Satan has continued his barrage of lies. That arrogant old devil even implied a lie in the temptations he presented to Jesus in the wilderness. Satan implied that if Jesus threw Himself off the temple roof, God would have to save Him. He was deceitfully trying to get Jesus to act out of disobedience one way or another.

The sad thing is that we have so easily followed Satan's pattern. Adam and Eve both were dishonest when confronted by God in the garden about why they were hiding. They were afraid of God's judgment. Adam tried to blame Eve, and Eve passed the buck to the snake, Satan. As we go through scripture we find lying is a problem in human nature that has continued to be passed down. Abraham lied about Sarah to protect himself from being murdered. Abraham's son Isaac did the same about Rebekah. Jacob, Isaac's son, was known for his deceit and trickery. It seems that one key reason people lie is out of fear. - fear of being honest and facing the consequences of the truth.

Paul confronted this fear as he wrote to the church in Galatia. They had turned away from the truth of the gospel and Paul had to rebuke them. In Galatians 4:16 he wrote, "Have I then become your enemy by telling you the truth?" He did not want them to believe Satan's lies of false doctrine so he had to face the possibility that they would be offended if he told them the truth.

Psalm 15:1 encourages all believers to tell the truth. It is a characteristic of those who abide close to the Lord. Let us make that our practice.

Taste Test:

Situational ethics is common in the TV shows or movies we watch. If we are not careful we will accept it as normal and right.

As you watch TV or a movie together, have a pen and paper handy for everyone.

- Jot down every time someone lies or acts dishonestly. After the show discuss why they lied and the consequences of their actions.
- How could they have benefited from telling the truth?

Scraping the Plate:

Read Psalm 15.

Compare the good qualities of verse 2 with the warnings against bad character in verse 3. Can you identify times when you see these qualities in the lives of people around you? Look at verse 4-5 and compare to honest and deceitful actions that are described. Sometimes honesty is carried out through actions as well as words. Discuss ways that is true in society.

Nanny's Chocolate Pie:

Jesus is the way, the truth, and the life. As the truth of God's Word He like His Father cannot lie. We want to be identified with our Lord and God as truthful in word and deed. We do not want our identity to be confused with Satan, the father of lies.

HUMILITY - the quality or state of mind where one does not think of themselves as better than others; lowliness of heart; meekness of spirit

"Live in harmony with one another. Do not be haughty, but associate with the lowly. Never be wise in your own sight". Romans 12:16

Scripture Text: John 13:3-17

The Prince and Pauper by Mark Twain, is a story that has been retold numerous times and ways. In this story, the Prince wanted to know the freedom of life without the responsibility of his crown, while the pauper wanted to experience the luxuries and power of the prince. My favorite twist of this classic story is when a person of power and influence sheds the robes of their position so that they might win the heart of another based solely on who they are as an individual. That was the case with Princess Jasmine in Disney's Aladdin. She longed for friendship and recognition outside of her position as princess.

Numerous people fall into the trap of doing the opposite, however. They think that having a position and role of importance raises them above others around them. They crave a title to accompany their name. They want an official seal or signet or ring to wear that displays their significance so that others can see.

Jesus had something to say about position. The Prince of Heaven, heir to the glory of the entire Universe, once laid aside His robes to wash the disciples feet. The very Son of God took on the role of the lowest servant in a household. John 13 tells this amazing story of Jesus' teaching His disciples a lesson on humility. Jesus clearly knew His position but did what no one else had volunteered to do when they first arrived. *"Jesus, knowing that the Father had given all things into his hands, and that he had come from God and was going back to God, rose from the supper. He laid aside his outer garments, and taking a towel, tied it around his waist. Then he poured water into a basin and began to wash the disciples' feet..." (vs 3-5a)*

This may not seem like a big deal to us but it was huge in significance to the disciples. The chore of washing another person's feet was an act of kindness and hospitality for guests in mid-eastern culture because of their walking about in sandals through the sand and dirt. It was always looked upon as a menial task that a lowly servant or slave would do. If a family had no servants, then the youngest capable child would be assigned the job. It surprised the disciples when they saw Jesus, their leader, begin washing their feet. Peter actually refused to let Jesus wash his feet until he understood the significance of the act.

Jesus then made this lesson clear. *"You call me Teacher and Lord, and you are right, for so I am. If I then, your Lord and Teacher, have washed your feet, you also ought to wash one another's feet."* Titles and position are not for glory and honor, rather they designate responsibility. Our responsibility as Jesus' followers is to love and serve one another, to share His truth with the world, and to live in peace and forgiveness. Only as we take a lowly position to do that, which pleases the Father, can we truly find the joy and significance we are looking for.

Taste Test:

Do you remember ever playing on a teeter-totter? One person has to go down in order for the other one to be raised up. When we do kind acts of assistance for another person, or help them without being forced, we lift them up. We are modeling Jesus' action in John 13. Jesus said, *"For I have given you an example, that you also should do just as I have done to you."*

- Explore ways in which you can help others around you with their needs. Maybe take on chores for others in the family and give them a needed break. One great idea is to write out certificates of kind deeds, in which a person offers a kind service to a family member:
  - ✓ One certificate for: Washing the Dishes for a Week.
  - ✓ One certificate for: One Car Wash
  - ✓ One certificate for: a Foot Massage
- Make up your own ideas and certificates and give them away this week.

Scraping the Plate:

Humility is the opposite of pride, which is a serious danger. God resists the proud but gives grace to the humble. Satan promotes pride. He was the first who let pride drive him into rebellion and sin. Humility is an act of trust and faith. When we realize that our identity is in God and that we are loved and accepted by Him for who we are, we are not worried about position and recognition among men. God gives us our significance and identity through our relationship with Jesus Christ. Is that what Jesus meant in John 13:16-17? Is your happiness found in Jesus?

Nanny's Chocolate Pie:

When we identify with Jesus as a Christ follower, humility is necessary as we begin the Christian walk. It takes repentance of sin, which prayerfully becomes a part of our fiber as we continue following Christ.

RIGHTEOUSNESS - free from guilt or sin; the quality of being morally good and obedient to religious laws and divine ethics

"Steadfast love and faithfulness meet; righteousness and peace kiss each other. Faithfulness springs up from the ground, and righteousness looks down from the sky. Yes, the Lord will give what is good,...Righteousness will go before him and make his footsteps a way." Psa. 85:10-13

Scripture Text: Romans 14:17

There are only five men described in scripture by the phrase, they were 'just' men. The phrase is not implying 'just' as in 'simply' men or 'only' men. The idea of the word 'just' is righteous in standing or to be in a good relationship because of one's character. It can refer to their relationship with God as well as their relationship with other people. Scripture here uses it as a synonym for the word righteous. The five men are Noah in Genesis 6:9, Joseph the husband of Mary in Matthew 1:19, Jesus in Matthew 27:19, John the Baptist in Mark 6:20, and Cornelius, the Centurion in Acts 10:22. What a high honor scripture gives to these individuals who as mere human men are attributed the same phrase that is used of Jesus. But what does it mean to be righteous, and how does righteousness appear in our relationships?

First, we consider our relationship with God and realize that no human person is righteous before Him. Romans 3:10 reminds us, *"None is righteous, no not one."* We can understand that by comparing Jesus' words in Mark 10:18, *"No one is good except God alone."* Paul explained in Romans 3:21-23, *"But now the righteousness of God has been manifested apart from the law, although the Law and the Prophets bear witness to it - the righteousness of God through faith in Jesus Christ for all who believe. For there is no distinction: for all have sinned and fall short of the glory of God,"*

To be righteous one has to be good enough, in the sense that they have never sinned. Only Jesus has ever lived up to that glorious standard. Every person falls short of that, yet God has made a way to change our standing. *"For our sake he made Him (Jesus) to be sin who knew no sin, so that in him we might become the righteousness of God."* 2 Corinthians 5:21 When we, by our faith, believe and trust in Jesus Christ as our Lord and Savior, God performs a legal transaction of exchanging our sin for His righteousness. He puts our sin with its judgment upon Jesus, who paid for it on the cross; and He gives us a clean record of innocence by which He declares that we are righteous. Noah, Joseph, John the Baptist, and Cornelius were righteous before God because by faith they believed.

The other aspect of righteousness is our relationship with others. Paul encouraged that all believers should live a lifestyle that clearly demonstrates the righteous work of God. Because God has made us righteous in our relationship with Him, we should strive to live apart from sin in our daily actions. In Romans 14:17 Paul was teaching the Roman believers to consider their behavior and how it affected others around them. Were they offending people who were weaker in their faith? Were they participating in activities that might lead others away from faith in Christ? His encouragement was that God's

Kingdom is more than religious duty and rituals; it is in our relationship with others.

The psalmist in Psalm 85:11-13 is celebrating the gift of God's righteousness and in response committing to be faithful. Noah, Joseph, John the Baptist, and Cornelius were men of good reputation toward the people with whom they lived, because of their faith in God.

Taste Test:

To demonstrate the work of God in righteousness:

- Take several sheets of blank paper (One for each person plus one more), your Bible, and a trashcan. Label one paper "Jesus' Sin." Label each of the other papers "My Sin." Place the Bible in the middle of the table with paper #1 entitled "Jesus' Sin" under it. Leave the paper entitled "Jesus' Sin" blank. Give every person one of the other papers. On it they should list any sins which they have committed at any time in their past (like: Lying, disobedience, anger, jealousy, etc). Let everyone place their list of sins on the table between them and the Bible. Read Isaiah 59:2. Explain that our sins separate us from God. (With older children you might want to go into more detail on what that separation means)
- Read 1 John 1:9 and Colossians 2:14. Explain that when we believe and trust in Jesus, we bring our sin to God by

confessing it to Him. God takes our sin away (You can remove their list and throw it into the trash can) and gives us Jesus' perfect record. (Pull out the list entitled Jesus' Sin and place it between every one and the Bible.) Now read Romans 8:1-10 and rejoice in God's gift of righteousness through Jesus Christ.

Scraping the Plate:

Read Romans 8:11-15 and 2 Peter 3:13-14. Because the marvelous work of God's graciousness has transformed us from being sinful into righteous individuals, we ought to be motivated to live a life pleasing to Him. What hope does our righteous standing with God provide according to Romans 8:11-15 and 2 Peter 3:13-14? What power does God provide to those who are now made righteous so that we can live pleasing to Him? Read Romans 12 and discuss some of the ways that we can live pleasing to God in our relationships with other people.

Nanny's Chocolate Pie:

Righteousness is the identity we have in heaven as God the Father views us through Jesus. Thank God our identity has changed in Christ from sinner to saint.

CONTENTMENT - the state of being happy regardless of situations and satisfied; having no need of more

"But godliness with contentment is great gain." 1 Timothy 6:6

Scripture Text: Philippians 4:11, 1 Timothy 6:1-19

The apostle Paul wrote to the Philippians when they had been gracious to support him financially. He stated that he had learned how to be content. *"Not that I am speaking of being in need, for I have learned in whatever situation I am to be content,"* Philippians 4:11. Paul knew what it was to have plenty and he had suffered the lack of necessities as well. He had been full and hungry. Because of these experiences he declared, *"I can do all things through Jesus Christ my Lord."*

I am reminded of the old Aesop's fable of the dog and the bone. As a dog went prancing off to bury a big bone he had been given, he crossed a small bridge. Looking down into the water below he saw his reflection. Thinking it was another dog with a bone, he growled and snarled. He could see the expression of growling and snarling on the face of the other dog in return. 'I want that bone too,' thought the greedy hound. But when he snapped at the dog in the water's reflection, he dropped the bone that was in his own mouth.

So it is with many people today. They see the possessions of others and are discontent. They want more. They want what others have. Rather than rejoicing in their own possessions as blessings from God and continuing to work toward the things they need, they slide into a pit of dissatisfaction. Like the dog in the fable, they lose the joy and comfort of God's provision.

Paul had learned the joy of trusting God in any situation. He looked beyond the present circumstances to understand God has more in store for His children. He encouraged us to look ahead to eternity and set our affections on things above. The hymn "Count Your Many Blessings" provides encouraging words. *When you look at others with their lands and gold, think that Christ has promised you His wealth untold. Count your many blessing money cannot buy, your reward in heaven not your home on high.*

Taste Test:

Many times our discontentment is evident in the 'fast food, instant gratification, multiple choice' society in which we live. We become picky and selective. Many kids refuse to eat what is laid out in front of them. One great way to learn contentment is to practice fasting.

- As a family skip a meal and use that time to pray for others who may not have even had a meal that day.
- Another way to fast is to abstain from a particular aspect of your meals, like dessert.
- Another suggestion is to serve a meal that would be common in a poor family, like rice and beans.

While practicing one of these suggestions, pray for those less fortunate than yourselves and thank the Lord for your blessings.

Scraping the Plate:

1 Timothy gives great encouragement to be content with the promise that godliness with contentment is great gain.

Read the context of that verse by reading all of 1 Timothy 6:1-10. What do you think is the motivation of these false teachers whom Paul is warning about in verse 5, 9-10? What do you think he means by our gain? What does being godly in Christ provide for us? Consider verse 19.

Nanny's Chocolate Pie:

Our contentment rests in who we are as God's children. We know that our Father cares for us and will provide for our needs.

LOVE - a feeling of strong affection as in romance, attraction, and devotion to another person or thing

"Greater love has no one than this, that someone lay down his life for his friends," John 15:13

Scripture Text: John 18:25-26, 21:1-19

Peter was faithful to Jesus Christ all the way to Jesus' death. However, at Christ's final hours Peter faltered and denied knowing Jesus three times. Jesus *said, "There is no greater love, than a man lay down his life for a friend."* On the same day that Peter denied knowing Jesus, Jesus laid His life down by dying on the cross of Calvary to save Peter. Sometime after Jesus rose from the dead, He appeared to the disciples on the seashore of Galilee. On the beach, with an inviting fire, Jesus had prepared breakfast. He called the disciples, including Peter, to join Him. During this incredible moment, Jesus reconciled with Peter. In other words, Jesus reached out to restore their friendship and the peace in their relationship by letting Peter know that he was forgiven.

Jesus asked Peter twice, *"Peter, do you love me?"* Jesus used the word for divine love, *agape*. Both times Peter responded, *"Yes, Lord."* But Peter could only use the word that relayed the depth of brotherly love. He felt as if he could not love with the same ability as God does because he had failed. He was right. A third time, though, Jesus asked, *"Peter, do you love me?"* This time Jesus also used the word for brotherly love, *phileo*, as Peter had done. I imagine tears came to Peter's eyes at this point as he knew he had denied Jesus three times, yet Jesus was accepting him in his weakness and forgiving him proportionately three times. Peter replied, *"Yes Lord, You know all things. You know that I love you."* Later, in Peter's life, we see how he proves his love for his Savior by laying down his life as well. He was hung on a cross upside down and crucified for sharing the love of Jesus and the gospel message with others.

Jesus said the greatest commandment is to love God with all your heart, soul, and mind. The second greatest commandment is to love your neighbor as yourself, Matthew 22:37-39. The greatest and most important attribute God wants for us is love. We should daily practice going out of our way to demonstrate His love for others because of how much He loves us.

Taste Test:

In the Baker family house, we would often play a game called the "Love Chair." In this game one person sits in a chair designated as the 'love chair' while everyone else in the family takes turns stating something they love about that individual. This continues until everyone has had a turn in the 'love chair.

Sometimes we would add different dimensions to it by varying the rules like: each person had to state that they loved the individual because that person had helped them in a specific way, or they loved that person because they reminded them of something else that they loved (i.e. - attribute of God, favorite food item, or a cartoon character) and why.

Consider making this a practice in your family.

Scraping the Plate:

Read 1 John 4:7 and discuss how God's love motivates us to love others. Can you see in your discussion that love apart from God is naturally selfish? Share how and why loving some people is hard and why?

Read 1 Corinthians 13:4-8 also and take time to discuss each aspect of this passage's description of divine love. Observe areas in your life where you have to confess like Peter that you cannot love like God does. Thank God for His unconditional love and ask Him to help you love more.

Nanny's Chocolate Pie:

God's children are known by their love for Him. However, it is God's love for us that motivates us to be pleasing to Him in all we do. We are His children; let us love others as much as we are loved.

RESPONSIBILITY - a duty or task that you are required or expected to do; the state of being accountable for what you are expected or have committed to accomplish

"Even a child makes himself known by his acts, by whether his conduct is pure and upright." Proverbs 20:11

Scripture Text: 1 Samuel 2:11-21, 3:1-21

Some children are born to privilege and others are born in poverty. Yet, regardless of their state in life, it seems many children today grow up with a sense of entitlement and lack of concern for others. A person's state in life, whether rich or poor, slave or free, and regardless of religion or ethnicity, does not change their responsibility to be honest in word or deed. *"Behold, You delight in truth in the inward being,..."* Psalm 51:6. There is a lack of responsibility toward doing and saying the right thing within today's culture that was not true in young Samuel's day.

Samuel's story is amazing and different. Most of us cannot relate to his circumstances. He was born into a blended home with a dad, a mom and a step-mom, and a lot of half brothers and sisters. His mother, who prayed for and loved him dearly, gave him up to live in the priest's home. She did not want to give him up, but she kept a promise to give him to the Lord because God had given him to her when she had been unable to have children. Scripture says he was 'lent' to the Lord, so it was as if Eli the priest adopted Samuel and raised him to serve the Lord in the tabernacle. Samuel was very young.

We do not know how long Samuel served the Lord before God spoke to him one night, we only know that Samuel had been growing up while serving in the tabernacle under the supervision of the priest, Eli. While other boys his age were out playing or spending time with their family and friends, Samuel worked. One night God spoke to Samuel and gave him grim news of Eli and his sons' judgment. Eli had two sons who were wicked liars and cheats. Eli had not restrained them from deceiving the people or from doing sinful acts, so God promised to judge them. God told young Samuel this solemn news, *"Then the Lord said to Samuel, 'Behold, I am about to do a thing in Israel at which the two ears of everyone who hears it will tingle. On that day I will fulfill against Eli all that I have spoken concerning his house, from beginning to end. And I declare to him that I am about to punish his house forever'."* Samuel was afraid to tell Eli what God had said, but Eli knew God had spoken to Samuel in the night and warned him that he should never hide God's messages. *"Samuel told him everything, and hid nothing from him,"* the scripture goes on to say. Samuel learned that it is a great responsibility to speak the truth, even if it is not pleasant. From that time on, Samuel spoke God's message to all Israel and continued to do what was right before God in service to others. God honored him because of it.

Many times we are faced with the responsibility of telling the truth when it is not easy. The truth can offend the hearts of those who are living in sin or do not want to know truth. Sometimes we carry the responsibility of doing what is difficult in work or service. We may feel like we are missing out on pleasures the rest of the world is enjoying. However, God has promised in Proverbs 20 that He knows what is best for us and He judges the innermost parts of the heart. God, in turn, will bless and preserve those who carry their responsibility seriously and truthfully.

Taste Test:

Do you ever want to lie when someone asks you a simple question? Maybe they ask you, 'How do I look today?' or 'Do you like this meal I prepared?' You don't want to hurt their feelings, yet you honestly don't think their outfit is attractive or the food they made is tasteful. Tell the truth kindly!

One of the greatest lessons in life is learning to be honest with our opinions while being tactful in expressing them.

- Set up some practice scenarios in your home where someone dresses up hideously and asks for others opinion.
- Practice ways of saying that the outfit is not becoming on them without sounding rude.
- Do the same with practice scenarios concerning meals.
- In the end, our loved ones will appreciate our honesty if it keeps them from serving a bland dish to guests or wearing an unsightly outfit in public.

Scraping the Plate:

Jesus bore the responsibility of sharing the good news of God's redemptive plan. However, that responsibility carried with it the need to be honest with everyone and to first warn them that they were sinners separated from God. In order to enjoy the blessing of eternal life and salvation's forgiveness of sin, Jesus said we must humbly repent and trust Him as Lord. Discuss how we as Christians can honestly and lovingly carry this responsibility to tell the lost world about their sinful condition and God's plan to save them. Will it offend some? Will some respond? Read Jude 1:21-25.

Nanny's Chocolate Pie:

Paul stated that we are ambassadors for Christ. We share an important responsibility because we have been born-again into great privilege. To ignore our responsibility to God's service is to deny our identity as privileged and blessed people.

COURAGE - the strength of heart to face and conquer fear or difficulties

"O Lord my God, in you do I take refuge; save me from all my pursuers and deliver me." Psalm 7:1

Scripture Text: Psalm 11

One of the most troubling of times is when you face persecution or trials from others. God does not promise that we will never face danger in this life. As a matter of fact, He says just the opposite. *"If they have persecuted me, they will also persecute you..."* Jesus said in John 15:20.

The Bible is full of stories of individuals who endured persecution. From Abraham and Lot to Joseph, Gideon, and the prophets, scripture teaches us to expect hardships at the hand of those who oppose our faith. The record of the nation of Israel when it faced national persecution also impresses upon us the extent of this hatred. Satan longs to kill, steal, and destroy, and he uses those who do not know the Lord to accomplish these goals.

David records his prayer in Psalm 11, about wanting to flee from the face of persecution. David experienced suffering at the hand of others many times. From the time, as a boy, he defeated the giant, Goliath, David suffered persecution because King Saul became jealous of the people's love for him. King Saul tried to kill him on several occasions. David then spend years fleeing for his life, hiding in caves, and living apart from his family while he waited for God to change his situation.

Later as King of Israel, David again had to flee from the palace; this time he fled because of persecution from his own rebellious son, Absalom. Absalom sought to kill his father and take over the kingdom. However, David recognizes, in his prayer, that running away is never a solution. David realized that the battle was spiritual rather than of human origin. Though human instruments are used by Satan to bring suffering or persecution, the foundations of God can never be destroyed. We need to know that God sees us and will keep His eye upon us to care for us in the midst of our trouble.

God has a bigger plan than our comfort and earthly wellbeing. He longs to use us to accomplish the eternal work of redemption, and many times God works through our suffering to display His grace to our persecutors. As a sculptor beats upon a large stone, chipping away to shape it into a marvelous piece of art, so God uses trials and even persecution to mold us into the very likeness of our Lord Jesus Christ.

David confesses these truths: that persecution will come and that God tries His own children through suffering, and that he will take refuge in God. Another way of saying that is, I will find my courage in God's presence and purpose. Know that no persecution can destroy you when you belong to God. Satan cannot kill you. All the persecution and suffering that come in this life are only meant as blows of the Master Sculptor's hammer to shape you into an eternal beautiful work of God.

Be courageous by knowing that God is with you, directing everything in your life, if you only trust Him.

Taste Test:

You may or may not be going through serious persecution at this time, but either way think about the workings of God as a sculptor chipping away on a slab of marble to create a beautiful statue of you.

- What are those things that need to be chipped away in your character that do not resemble the Lord Jesus Christ?
- Retell the story of Joseph or Esther at a family devotion time and modernize it, putting each person in the family as the main character.
- How would you respond to persecution?

Scraping the Plate:

Read excerpts from the *Foxes Book of Martyrs* or from *Voice of the Martyrs* publications. Discuss how saints of God have suffered over the centuries for their faith and how God has used their suffering. Pray for those who face suffering now and pray for courage for when you might have to face it.

Nanny's Chocolate Pie:

Suffering persecution or going through trials is part of who we are as God's children. He promised that we would share in the reproach of Christ. Our identity includes displaying the grace of God as we endure those difficulties with courage.

KINDNESS - the quality or state of being affectionate, gentle, and helpful to others; the act of wanting to and enjoying doing good deeds to make others happy

"As we therefore have opportunity, let us do good unto all men, especially unto those who are of the household of faith." Galatians 6:10

Scripture Text: Leviticus 19:34

As God prepared the children of Israel to live in the land of Canaan, He wanted their character to be different than the wicked people who lived there before them. The various Canaanite peoples had fallen into such evil sin that God was going to drive them out of the land and give it to Israel. God wanted His people to behave in ways that would honor Him. He made plans that they would even show kindness to the strangers who passed through the land. They were to not harvest all of their crops in harvest time, just so travelers could gather something to eat.

In Jesus' day he taught the same type of kindness when He told the story of the Good Samaritan. Samaritans were people who were considered unworthy people by the Jews, but this Samaritan was the only one willing to help. Here was a man who, while traveling across the country, took time out of his trip to help a stranger who had been beaten and robbed. Jesus even encouraged His followers to love their enemies, and go the extra mile when they were asked to help someone.

Late one afternoon my family was traveling home from a distant city in our old SUV. We were still almost 100 miles away from home when the vehicle broke down. We pulled over to the side of the road and tried to call for help, but couldn't reach anyone. One person stopped to help us. He gave me a ride into the nearest town so I could make arrangements for a mechanic and wrecker. While I was in town doing that, another person stopped at the SUV and gave my wife money to help pay for the repairs. Then some friends from church drove all the way to the place where our car had broken down and gave us a ride home. These various acts of kindness were wonderful and heartwarming and came when we were in need.

Since then my family tried to repay those acts of kindness by doing similar acts of kindness to others. Galatians 6:10 encourages us to do good and be kind whenever we have opportunity.

Taste Test:

Many people have an emergency kit in case they ever need it. However, have you ever thought of making a kit that provides items that you could use to offer assistance to others if the opportunity arises?

- Make a list of things that you might like to put in it, like extra cash, a map, old clothes to work in case you had to change a tire, water, etc.
- Use a plastic storage container to store the items and your kit is complete!

Scraping the Plate:

Discuss times in your past when people have gone out of their way to be kind to you. Tell stories of when you know of those types of examples in others. Why is kindness such a dynamic way to display your Christian faith?

Nanny's Chocolate Pie:

God showed His kindness by graciously providing forgiveness and salvation. The Fruit of the Holy Spirit is kindness. We should be identified as Christians by the kindness we practice as well.

CHAPTER 3

Belonging

- Courage
- Hospitality
- Joyfulness
- Kindness
- Loyalty
- Awareness
- Honesty
- Patience
- Righteousness
- Determination
- Resourcefulness

COURAGE - the strength of heart to face and conquer fear or difficulties

"Have I not commanded you? Be strong and courageous. Do not be frightened, and do not be dismayed, for the Lord your God is with you wherever you go." Joshua 1:9

Scripture Text: Daniel 3:1-30

When the Lord wants us to take something to heart and trust Him, He repeats it. Over 350 times the words *"do not fear"* appear in the Bible. So after such repetition we should know we have nothing to fear, God will protect us.

In the book of Daniel, we find the story of Shadrach, Meshach, and Abednego. These three Hebrew men were in captivity in the land of Babylon during the reign of King Nebuchadnezzar. The King issued a law saying everyone in the entire kingdom had to bow down and worship a statue that he had built. The statue was of him. The law stated that when a certain song would be played, everyone was to bow before this statute in reverence. It added that those who refused to bow would be thrown into a fiery furnace.

Shadrach, Meshach, and Abednego courageously chose not to bow down even though they knew the consequences. They had learned from their own Hebrew laws as children to honor and obey God first. The second commandment God gave the Hebrew people when He called them to follow Him states, *"You shall have no other gods before me, you shall not make for yourself a carved image of anything that is in heaven above, or that is in the earth beneath, or that is in the water under the earth. You shall not bow down to them or serve them, for I the Lord your God am a jealous God."* Exodus 20:3-5.

Knowing this commandment, these three brave men refused to bow down to Nebuchadnezzar's image. The King gave them a second chance when he saw that they didn't bow the first time, but they still refused to bow staying faithful to the one true God. Infuriated, King Nebuchadnezzar ordered them thrown into the furnace. However, God protected them and the fire didn't even singe their clothing.

Now we may not all face death because of our belief in Jesus and because of our faith in God as the one true God as Shadrach, Meshach, and Abednego, but we are called to spread the news of Jesus Christ and His gift of eternal life. Sharing the good news of Christ can be hard and terrifying at times, but we must know that God is always with us even if we face embarrassment or persecution. We will be rewarded for our obedience.

Living in the midst of people who do not always agree with our Christian beliefs causes conflict. They do not understand our trust in God nor our worship. Our faith however, causes a desire in us to want them to believe the same way that we do, because we want others to know Jesus and spend eternity in Heaven. Here is where courage comes in; we must not compromise our faith nor live in a way that does not emphasize our worship of the true and living God. We must courageously live for God among them and tell them about Jesus. There is no greater joy than leading someone to faith in Jesus Christ.

Taste Test:

Watch the movie "Courageous" and discuss together how you can demonstrate your courage for God in your community and family. Read a missionary biography together of one of the heroes of our faith who endured great trails to spread the gospel like: Hudson Taylor, Adoniram Judson, David Brainerd, or Erik Little.

Scraping the Plate:

- Discuss times when you are put to the test at work or school to stay true to your faith when others who claim to believe compromise.
- Discuss the nature of the lost - as to why they have no control over their sinful nature until they are transformed in Christ; therefore, they are in need of our witness.
- How can you boldly take a stand to share your faith through your church work or family?

Sunday Roast:

When you have a mighty God backing you up with His presence and promises, fear is driven away. Courage is a gift of belonging to Him.

HOSPITALITY - being generous and friendly in treatment of visitors; the activity of providing food and refreshment for people who are guests

"Above all keep loving one another earnestly, since love covers a multitude of sins. Show hospitality to one another without grumbling." 1 Peter 4:8-9

Scripture Text: Luke 7:37-50

I once knew an elderly lady who visited the nursing homes in her rural community of Goldthwaite, Texas every week. She would walk from room to room visiting and trying to provide a sense of joy and encouragement to the people who lived there. Even though she herself was getting up in years, she baked cookies every week to deliver to these people who could no longer do such a simple task for themselves. She continued this simple act of hospitality and kindness for years, until she herself entered the nursing home at the age of 104.

Luke 7:37-50 tells an amazing account of a time when a woman showed great hospitality to Jesus. It was customary in Hebrew culture, that when people visited another's home three things would be done for them. First, a servant would wash their feet to cleanse away the dust from their travels. Secondly, the host would greet them with a kiss on the cheek. Finally, they would anoint (pour oil on the head of) their guests with spice-scented olive oil as a mark of welcome.

The Pharisee in this story invited Jesus to dine with him but provided none of the customary acts of hospitality. Many of the Pharisees did not believe in Jesus and were seeking ways to discredit Him among the people. However, a woman who was known as a sinner among the people entered the Pharisees home during the dinner. She began to weep and wash Jesus' feet with her tears and hair. She then kissed His feet and anointed them with the ointment. The Pharisee was horrified by her intrusion and thought that Jesus was wrong for letting her do all of this. Jesus frankly confronted the Pharisee and challenged him with a story of a rich man and two debtors. One debtor owed a lot while the other only a little. Both men were forgiven of their debt. Jesus asked the Pharisee which debtor would love their gracious benefactor the most.

The moral of that story is: Those to whom much has been forgiven will love much. The Pharisee was not willing to receive the forgiveness of his sins because he did not think he needed it. He remained selfish and indignant. The woman, on the other hand, was so grateful that Jesus was willing to forgive her of her sins; she wanted to pour out all the love and hospitality she could on Him.

Taste Test:

Jesus taught us that what we do to bless others, we do as if unto Him.

If you are grateful for what Jesus has done in your life by making forgiveness available and by blessing you, why don't you plan to visit those in need to provide a blessing to them. There may be a nursing home close to you that you could visit to provide encouragement and maybe even cookies. You might visit the jail or a homeless shelter and share the gospel while assisting in food distribution.

Scraping the Plate:

Discuss 1 Peter 4:8-9 and how the story of this woman's hospitality in Luke 7 must have been a great influence on Peter as he wrote these words. Would you be able to say that your hospitality is recognizable by others? How can you make it more honorable to the Lord?

Sunday Roast:

When a person embraces the concept that they belong to a loving and infinite God, they long to share His love with others. Being hospitable is one way to show His love.

JOYFULNESS - the feeling of great happiness or delight evoked by wellbeing, success, or good fortune

"May you be strengthened with all power, according to His glorious might, for all endurance and patience with joy." Colossians 1:11

Scripture Text: Exodus 14-15

Many times God allows our faith to be tested or He puts us in situations where we must depend upon Him. Years ago, in a small central Texas town I struggled as a young pastor in getting a group of young people to embrace faith. They believed in God and many of these young people already trusted the Lord Jesus as their Savior. However, the idea of trusting Him by faith for all things was abstract. As I prayed for God's guidance, He led me to Psalm 18:28-29. It was as if God was saying, "if these young people will commit to trust me, I will empower them more than they have ever known before". I gave them that challenge at the beginning of the school year at a church sponsored event. They accepted the challenge and the year was full of surprises. The football team went deeper into the playoffs than they had gone in years. The girls and boys basketball teams did even better. The school's one act play went to regionals and their UIL team had students who went to state. The year was not without difficulties in any of these endeavors, but can you imagine the joy these young people realized in light of God's favor.

The Israelites experienced the joy of trusting God in difficult circumstances. Freshly departed from Egypt, this band of freed slaves found themselves caught between the Red Sea and an imposing Egyptian army. They either blamed Moses for putting them in harm's way, or they whined about their decision to leave Egypt. God gave them a message to trust Him and watch for His deliverance. Moses then raised His staff, the Red Sea parted in the middle, and the relieved Israelites scampered across to the other side. After God closed the waters upon the pursuing Egyptian army and they were defeated, joy swept across the Israelite nation.

Moses' sister, Miriam, led the women in a dance and song of victory.

> *" Sing to the Lord because He is worthy of great honor.*
> *He has thrown the horse and the rider into the sea."*

What joy! Their joy was not just in being rescued or delivered. Rather, the joyfulness of the occasion was found in God's faithfulness and presence. Truly there is no greater joy than knowing by experience that God loves you and is working for you.

Taste Test:

I cannot promise that God will work in your life as a family the same way He chose to bless one group of young people years ago in that small town. I can promise that if you seek Him with all your heart and choose to trust His guidance, He will lead you into seeing His hand of care and direction.

Why don't you make a family prayer journal, listing the needs, battles, and/or challenges that you face?

- Begin praying for God's guidance and commit to be obedient to His direction as you read His Word.
- Write in the journal any scripture God leads you to study and meditate upon.
- Record God's hand as you see it over the next few months or year.

Scraping the Plate:

Turn the story in Exodus 14-15 around as if the Israelites had not trusted God and not followed Moses. Discuss what their fate might have been and what would have been the state of their joy. Many people derive their happiness only when things are going well or they are winning. The world is full of athletes, fans, business people, and everyday folks that watch their happiness rise and fall like a yo-yo, because they don't know how to trust God in difficult circumstances and wait upon Him. Share how waiting upon God to work things out according to His timing leads to consistency in joy. "*Then I will go to the altar of God, to God my exceeding joy, and I will praise you with the lyre, O God, my God.*" Psalm 43:4.

Sunday Roast:

Truly there is no greater joy than knowing by experience that God loves you and is working for you simply because you belong to Him by faith.

KINDNESS

- the quality or state of being affectionate, gentle, and helpful to others; the act of wanting to and enjoying doing good deeds to make others happy

"Be kindly affectionate to one another with brotherly love, in honor giving preference to one another." Romans 12:10

Scripture text: Philippians 2:26-30

Geese are interesting creatures to watch. When they fly in their famous V-formation they are drafting off of the leader. They also are actually taking turns at the lead to make it easier on all of them to fly greater distances. The lead goose serves as point, cutting through the wind current, while the others draft off of him. Occasionally, the leader will pull off and move to the back of the V, letting another goose move into the lead spot. It is hard and tiring being in the front. Interestingly, all the geese in the back consistently honk at the leader as if to encourage him to keep going.

Sometimes a goose gets injured or sick. If one has to drop out of the V and land because he cannot continue, two other geese will join him. These geese never leave the sick one's side until he recovers or dies.

Paul knew of this type of kindness in the friendship of Epaphroditus. Epaphroditus was a member of the church at Philippi. He came to minister and care for Paul on behalf of the church while Paul was in prison. During his stay in Rome where Paul was lodged, Epaphroditus became deathly ill. However, his primary concern was still to care for Paul and serve him on behalf of his fellow believers back at home. He did not even want those in Philippi to know he was ill because he did not want to worry them. He was always thinking of the best interests of his friends as well as Paul.

Paul honored Epaphroditus when he wrote to the church at Philippi. Paul encouraged them to rejoice with Epaphroditus when he returned home, because he had been such an encourager and caregiver to Paul. Paul may have thought of Epaphroditus when he taught the church in Rome about kindness.

Taste test:

Make two lists as you discuss kindness.

- Write the first list of those people who have been especially kind to you over the years. List the ways in which they demonstrated their kindness.
- Write the second list of people you know who need an act of kindness shown to them.
- Write a thank you card or call someone who had shown kindness to you.
- Then choose the person to whom you can be kind to this week and think of ways to show it to them.

Scraping the Plate:

Read 2 Samuel 9:1-13. Discuss how David was kind to Mephibosheth.

Compare that act of kindness to God's kindness to all of us in Christ Jesus.

How are we like Mephibosheth and God like David? How can we be more like David in this story?

Sunday Roast:

Kindness is a fruit of God's Holy Spirit. Our kindness to others is evidence of the One to whom we belong.

LOYALTY - a feeling of strong support for someone or something

But Elisha said, "As the Lord lives, and as you yourself live, I will not leave you." - 2 Kings 2:2

Scripture text: Acts 20:16-20, 36-38

The apostle Paul was a missionary sent out by the early church in Antioch to spread the good news of the gospel. His ministry had many difficulties, and he had faced many adversities (enemies) at times. He made three journeys throughout Asia and was led by God's Spirit to return to Jerusalem with an offering to support the struggling church there. The Holy Spirit had also impressed him that it would be his last journey, for the people who opposed him had planned to have him arrested or worse.

In Acts 20:16-38 we read where Paul passed by Asia Minor sailing back from Greece to Jerusalem. Facing great danger and opposition to his preaching about faith in Jesus Christ, Paul decided not to stop in Ephesus even though he had dear friends who lived there. Yet for all the friends he had there, he also had great enemies.

He sent a message to those friends that his ship would dock further south. These precious friends of Paul's came from Ephesus to meet and support him. They were loyal to Paul because he had loved them enough to preach and teach them about Jesus. Many of these people had been saved out of sin (became believers) under Paul's ministry. Their loyalty was seen as they hugged, kissed, and wept over Paul's leaving. They were genuinely concerned for his safety, but they also wanted to see God accomplish His will through Paul. They were not only loyal to Paul as caring friends, they desired God's will and best for him. Therefore they prayed with him for those very things. Loyal friends support each other, care for each other, and pray for each other.

The Taste Test:

About fifteen minutes into the Disney movie, *Pooh's Great Search for Christopher Robin,* Christopher poses a question to Pooh wondering what the world would be like if they were ever separated. Pooh philosophizes that could never happen, and Christopher Robin then declares, "I will always be with you." In another movie, *The Lord of the Rings* series, the hobbit, Sam, refuses to leave the side of his friend and fellow hobbit, Frodo. Sam keeps his word and stays true to Frodo throughout their entire treacherous journey.

These movie clips demonstrate the idea of loyalty. Watch one or both of them again and discuss how you see this trait in the characters.

Scraping the Plate:

How can you show loyalty to your friends and family?

How does this verse relate to loyalty, Proverbs 17:17? "*A friend loves at all times, and a brother is born for adversity.*"

Loyalty is a characteristic of God himself. Jesus said He would never leave us not forsake us. He is always working for our good and eternal wellbeing. Those who belong to God through faith in Jesus can share the trait of loyalty by being supportive and helpful, by demonstrating their love, and by praying for each other. Discuss and choose a way that you can be a help to a friend or family member. Plan out how you want to show your family you love them. Pray for each other or for a friend right now.

Sunday Roast:

As the family of God we will belong to each other for all eternity. We should be encouraged to faithfully support each other now as we have opportunity.

AWARENESS - knowing and recognizing that something exists; finding wonder in and noticing the world around you

"The hearing ear and the seeing eye, the Lord has made them both. Love not sleep, lest you come to poverty; open your eyes, and you will have plenty of bread." Proverbs 20:12-13

Scripture Text: 2 Kings 6:8-23

Is seeing believing? Or is believing seeing? Hebrews 11:1 says, *"Now faith is the assurance of things hoped for, the conviction of things not seen."* You will see the things of God only when and if you choose to believe and trust Him. God, in His graciousness, blesses us at times with accounts and experiences in which He allows us to see His works to encourage our faith. He wants us to *"open our eyes"* as the proverb states that we might see the provision of God.

Elisha needed to trust God for the provision of protection and guidance when he was under attack by the Syrian King. The story in 2 Kings is of a terroristic King wanting to conquer Israel. Elisha, the prophet, kept warning the King of Israel in advance, of Syria's attacks. He even revealed where the attacks would happen. This destroyed the Syrian's plan every time. The King of Syria then decided to attack the prophet of God to put an end to his dilemma.

Early one morning Elisha's servant was both shocked and terrified when he went outside to discover their small city surrounded by the entire Syrian army. *"Alas, my master! What shall we do?"* he exclaimed to Elisha as he ran back inside the house. Elisha simply and calmly prayed to his Father in Heaven, "*O Lord, open his eyes that he may see.*" Then the servant looked outside to see God's chariots of fire encompassing Elisha for protection.

As the servant's eyes were opened, God blinded the Syrian armies' eyes. Elisha delivered the blind army to the king of Israel, God gave them back their sight, and the king sent them home to Syria. All eyes were opened spiritually to see the power of God as He provided deliverance for Israel and protection for Elisha.

Was God's protection there all along even when the servant could not see it? Was God's power able to deliver even though the Syrian army did not believe it? Yes! Emphatically, God's protection and power were there. Many were blinded by their own faithlessness. God allowed their eyes to be opened that they might see His works and choose to believe.

God wants us to grow in faith by being aware of His works. Jesus used this method many times in His ministry. When he healed, it was not only for the comfort of those who were diseased and lame. He healed and performed miracles so that many would believe on His name. Faith is an awareness of the work of God. Additionally, the more we trust in Him by faith, the more of His works we will see.

There was a time in my family's life when we struggled financially. The children were young and the church in which I ministered at was unable to pay my salary. I had no idea where I would get the resources to buy food for our next week's meals. I grew up poor so my obvious thought was to find more work; take a second (or third) job. Many times God had provided that way in the past. This time, however, God opened my eyes in a different way. A phone call came. A church member needed to get rid of a bunch of chickens. "Would you like to take a few of these off my hands?" he asked. We chopped, plucked, and cleaned chickens for hours, but my family had meat on the table for many days. God blessed and I was made aware of a new work of God's provision. Through that experience, I have learned to trust that God will provide in a variety of ways. I need only to open my eyes and see the glory of the Lord.

Taste Test:

Take a blow dryer, point it straight up into to air, and turn it on high. Place a Ping-Pong ball in the current of air above the dryer. The Ping-Pong ball should balance 'magically' in the current of air with nothing touching it. You can even pass your finger quickly under it and it will stay suspended in the current. Do you 'see' the current of air? No, but you know it is there because you are causing it to occur through the blow dryer. God is the cause of many things we do not see, *"For by Him were all things created, that are in Heaven and that are in the earth, visible and invisible,..."* Colossians 1:16a. Make a list of things that we do not see on a daily basis that God has created by which we are blessed. (Wind, energy, love,...)

Scraping the Plate:

Read 2 Kings 5, 6, and 7. These are some of the most amazing stories of God's provision, yet saddest stories of people's spiritual blindness.

- What caused Naaman to be closed to trusting God and what opened his eyes?
- How could Gahazi, the servant of Elisha, see the hand of God in healing Naaman yet be closed to the power of God to provide for himself and stoop to lying and trickery?
- After God delivered the Israelites from Syria once, why did they refuse to trust God when under attack again?
- How could women stoop to cannibalism of their own children, and the King blame the man of God?
- Why were they so surprised in chapter seven when God rescued them?
- Discuss how being aware of God and His works in our lives will help us in not making the same mistakes as others. It will also help us trust and see the power of God revealed around us.

Sunday Pot Roast:

When a person chooses to trust and believe in Christ as Savior, they become a child of God. Belonging to God instills the awareness of His presence and the assurance His of continual provision.

HONESTY - the state of being and actions of being good and truthful; free from fraud or deception; not hiding the truth about someone or a situation; not being willing to deceive

"But speaking the truth in love, may grow up in all things into Him who is the head - Christ." Ephesians 4:15

Scripture Text: 1 Kings 22:1-40

Though we know we should always tell the truth, there are those in culture that say honesty should be based upon the situation and how it will affect others. Sometimes telling the truth is hurtful because telling the truth might offend someone else's feelings or beliefs.

Remember the silly children's story of the Emperor and his new set of clothes by Hans Christian Anderson. The Emperor wanted a new and dashing outfit to wear for an upcoming event. He commissioned two tailors to make an outfit for him. These tailors swindled the King by promising the finest suit of clothes made from a fabric invisible to anyone who was unfit for his position. The Emperor's servants could not see the clothing when the King tried it on, but refused to say anything out of fear that it would reveal they were unfit for their position. They all pretended they could see a dashing outfit for fear of offending the monarch.

As the dishonest tailors pretended to help dress the Emperor on the day of the parade, they bragged about how fine he looked. The Emperor too, did not want to reveal the fact that he could not see the new clothing, because that would expose his unfitness to be king. The Emperor then paraded through the town wearing nothing at all but a smile, while all the townsfolk gawked in alarm, but said nothing. They applauded out of polite respect for the king, but fear held their tongues. Finally, from the crowd a young child, unaware of the pretense, blurted out that the king was naked. How embarrassing as both the Emperor's nakedness and pride were exposed.

Micaiah was a prophet of God in the days of wicked King Ahab of Israel. He told the truth and was thrown into prison because that truth displeased the King. Later Ahab wanted to go to war and reclaim a section of land that the Syrian army had taken from them. He inquired of all the prophets who represented the pagan gods and these men encouraged him to go – fight - win. However, the King of Judah was in allegiance with King Ahab, and he insisted to hear from a prophet of the true and living God, Jehovah. Micaiah was summoned from the prison. At first, he sarcastically responded by agreeing with the false prophets. King Ahab, sensing his sarcasm, demanded he speak truthfully. Then Micaiah spoke honestly the message that the Lord had revealed to him. If Ahab went to battle, he would surely die. He exposed that God had allowed a lying spirit to move among all of the false prophets to persuade King Ahab to go to battle. God was bringing about King Ahab's just end. Micaiah's prophecy came true exactly as he said it would. Even though it was hard to tell the truth, Micaiah did so because he remained faithful to the God to whom he belonged.

Taste Test:

Play a "Truth-or-Dare" game to safely practice the reality of telling the truth or suffering the consequences of dishonesty. Have each family member write down 3 questions that they want the others to answer, like:

"Do you really like ________________ for dinner?

"What is your opinion of Grandma's new hair color?" (Or some lady in church)

"Do you think I sing well enough to be on American Idol?"

Have an unusual food dish or baby food flavor ready for the ones who choose dare over truth. Take turns giving each person the opportunity to ask another person one of his or her questions. The person asked has the option of answering the question honestly or taking the dare to eat the nasty food item. Make certain everyone has the opportunity to both ask and answer questions. Emphasize that telling the truth may be hard, and it may even be difficult, but it is always right.

Scraping the Plate:

Read 1 Kings 22:1-40 again. Why did Micaiah the prophet not want to tell the King the truth at the beginning and rather sarcastically agreed with the false prophets? Why is telling the truth always important regardless of the consequences?

Hebrews 6:18 and Titus 1:2 reveal something of the nature of God. What is it? Should we base our behavior on what God is like in His nature or on what culture says?

Sunday Roast:

The way we communicate, clearly lets people know to whom we belong. We should be honest because we belong to our Father in Heaven.

PATIENCE - the state of being able to remain calm and not annoyed when waiting for a long time; maintaining an inner peace when dealing with problems or difficult people

"Count it all joy, my brothers when you meet trials of various kinds, for you know that the testing of your faith produces steadfastness (patience - KJV)." James 1:2-3

Scripture Text: James 5:7-11

It takes but a moment for an accident to take place. In seconds one can be broken and damaged by the events of tragedy. In the early 1980s, a friend of our family was involved in an automobile accident that crushed her body and stole the life of her little girl. This lady, who was in her early forties, was already a widow with two daughters. After the accident she had the long, wearisome ordeal ahead of recovery while grieving the loss of her young daughter and worrying about who would help provide for her teenage daughter.

When I served as pastor in central Texas I looked out my dining room window one mid-autumn morning to see fire trucks and emergency vehicles arriving across the street. I noticed a fire in the trees. I ran across the street to see if I could be of any assistance. I was quickly ushered into a neighbor's house to speak to a distraught young boy and his mom. The lady's husband was in a lift trimming trees near power lines. He accidently raised it into a power line and the electric current caused the gasoline can he had with him to explode. The lady and her son stood watching in horror as their lives were immediately changed by this tragedy.

Accidents and tragedies are common to this world. I have seen the tragedy of disease as it steals lives. I have stood with families at the graveside of teenagers killed on motorcycles. I have hugged parents who lost children, and I have been to storm torn communities. I have counseled those going through divorce and those who struggled through poverty. However, how people respond to tragedies is quite different.

Job is recognized in scripture for his patience in the midst of tragedy. James 5:11 acknowledges that point. Job was a just man, spiritually, and well accomplished in life financially. Tragedy is no respecter of persons. One day disaster struck his life in various forms. His cattle and flocks were all stolen by marauding mercenaries; during the same time frame a wind storm destroyed the house where all ten of his children were gathered for a celebration, killing them all. Job went from prosperous to pitiful in a moment. Yet Job never blamed God nor stopped trusting in Him. He even praised God in the midst of the pain, though probably with tears pouring down his cheeks. Job remembered that God's promises entail His abiding presence and strength in the midst of this world. Those promises provide hope for an eternal home apart from tragedy. Job's heart was firmly established in his relationship of trust toward God. Rather than run from God, he ran to Him.

The lady, who lost her little girl in the accident, recovered slowly from her lacerations and broken bones. A church family sheltered her teenage daughter during her recovery. She was back in church as soon as possible and through a scarred smile, praised the Lord for His providence. She confessed that she could trust that her husband was enjoying their little girl being home with him. The family, whose husband died in the fire, came to know and trust in the Lord as their Savior. The community rallied around them to help them relocate and start life again. Only as we trust in the Lord through our trials will we see the joy that eventually comes through His grace. That is James' encouragement - consider it a joyous event that God is with you and directing you through your trials and tragedies because you know He will see you through them.

Taste Test:

Regardless where you live, there is bound to be those around you who have recently experienced tragedy of some type, maybe within your own family. Looking at other people's tragedies can give us a different perspective than looking at our own. Share the events that others have gone through and examine how God might be using that tragedy to provide His grace into their lives.

- Discuss tragedies of current events from around the world.
- Does God really care? That is the questions some individuals ask when experiencing a discouraged spirit or struggling faith.
- How can God use you to bring joy into their lives? Pray for those families together now.

Scraping the Plate:

Read James 5:7-11 again. Verse 7 reminds us that we are in the Lord's providential hand, like the farmer waiting on the rains for his crops, yet verse 9 implies it is easy for us to complain. It specifically says we complain against each other. Why do we so easily compare our situation with that of others and want to complain when someone else has it 'better' than we perceive that we do? How is envy dangerously tied to a lack of faith as we complain? Compare this to Numbers 11:1 and 14: 1-35.

Sunday Roast:

Jesus promised that this world would hate us because it hated Him. Our persecution and suffering is part of belonging to Christ, but it comes with the promise that if we will endure, we will be saved. The completion of our salvation in glory with rewards awaits those who are patient.

RIGHTEOUSNESS - the quality of being morally good and obedient to religious laws and divine ethics; free from guilt or sin

" The Lord has made known His salvation; His righteousness He has revealed in the sight of the nations." Psalm 98:2

Scripture Text: Luke 3:1-4

"Just take it," Barney said to Tom, "no one will know and it's only fair."

The two boys were walking home from school. As they passed by the manicured home of a well-to-do classmate, they had noticed a basketball lying beside the curb. Tom loved basketball but did not have one of his own with which to practice or play.

Barney encouraged him again, "They probably have several more balls and won't even miss it. It's not right that someone who doesn't even care enough about their things to pick 'em up should have so much."

Tom thought about that phrase 'not right.' His parents had taught him that he should be more concerned with being righteous than being right. "No, I can't take it. That would be stealing, and stealing displeases God. Just because it would make things appear right by making the number of balls we have more fair, it would not be right according to God's laws." Tom had learned a great lesson in living out one's righteousness.

John the Baptist was a great example of righteousness in the Bible. He left following the examples of the religious leaders of his day because they did not walk in righteousness. They always wanted to appear as though they were right with God by dressing a certain way, praying long public prayers, and forcing people to pay tithes and offerings. However, John saw that they behaved quite contrary to their professed beliefs. They cheated the people and did not show genuine love or kindness.

John left the city and lived in the desert just so he could draw near to God personally. He strived hard to live in such a way that pleased God. Then he began to preach in the wilderness, calling the people to turn from their sin and ask for God's forgiveness. He promised that the Messiah would come and make them truly righteous before God by forgiving their sin. John also baptized everyone who repented of their sins in the Jordan River. Not long after that, Jesus arrived at the Jordan. John pointed Him out to everyone and declared, *"Behold the Lamb of God who takes away the sin of the world."*

Righteousness is the condition of all believers when they trust in Jesus and receive His forgiveness for their sin as a gift from God. Because of that gift of salvation, believers, like Tom, try to live in obedience to God's commandments and try to please Him.

Taste Test:

- Scan through a newspaper together or look at online news clips about events going on in the world and your community.

- Pick out articles and categorize them into "righteous living" and "selfish living." Many people try to make life "fair" like Barney suggested.
- Why does that kind of fairness fall under the category of selfishness most times?
- How do those stories that you categorized as "righteous living" demonstrate behavior that is pleasing to God?

Scraping the Plate:

Read Psalm 98:2. Discuss how God is righteous in all His ways. What did David mean when he prayed in Psalm 5:8 for God to lead him in righteousness? Is that also what the apostle Paul meant in 1 Corinthians 15:33-34?

Sunday Roast:

We behave rightly because we have been declared righteous. Belonging to God, as His children, produces the motive necessary to behave in a manner, which pleases Him. We cannot earn His grace, love, or redemption - He gives it. Having received his grace, by faith, we live accordingly.

DETERMINATION - the quality that makes you continue trying to do or achieve something that is difficult

"I press toward the goal for the prize of the upward call of God in Christ Jesus." Philippians 3:14

Scripture Text: 2 Timothy 2:4-6

Our family has always made it a habit of trying to stay fit and exercising. Recently a friend and I set a goal of doing 5000 push-ups in as little amount of time as possible. We took turns in set amounts until we accomplished one thousand. Then we would take short breaks and start the next set of one thousand. After two and a half hours we accomplished our goal, but it was far from easy. After just the first thousand my wrists were hurting and I had to wrap them for support. After two thousand our hands were beginning to hurt also, but we pushed on. After four thousand, we were both completely soaked in sweat, and we were extremely tired. We knew we would be disappointed if we did not reach our goal, so we continued. We fought through the exhaustion and pain to finish the final one thousand.

Paul tells the Philippians to press on toward their goal for the prize of the upward call of God in Christ Jesus. Our goal as Christians is to be like Christ and bring glory to God. We should be determined to reach the goal of being Christ-like. The idea in scripture of Christian atonement comes from the idea of being "at-one" with God. The great beauty of the triune nature of God is unity: God the Father, Son, and Spirit operating and existing in perfect harmony. God blesses us with that same relationship through Jesus Christ in that we are made one with God. Our goal then should be to act and live our lives with that unity in mind. Our actions and thoughts should be Christ-like. "*Have this mind among yourselves, which is yours in Christ Jesus,*" Paul encouraged, "*Do all things without grumbling or disputing, that you may be blameless and innocent, children of God without blemish in the midst of a crooked and twisted generation, among whom you shine as lights in the world.*"

2 Timothy 2:4-6 tells us that no soldier gets entangled in civilian pursuits, since his aim is to please the one who enlisted him. An athlete is not crowned unless he competes according to the rules. It is the hard-working farmer who ought to have the first share of his own crops. These are all examples Paul used to encourage Timothy to stay determined in his goal of being Christ-like in character and actions.

Taste Test:

Set a goal for this week. Choose a goal that is realistic and worthy whether it be running and working out, fasting and spending time with the Lord, or helping others.

Include in your plan the steps as to how you will accomplish your goal concluding with how this project will enrich your character to be more like Christ.

For Example:

- Goal - Run/walk 3 miles - 3 times this week.

- Plan - Get up early before other activities start on Monday, Wednesday, and Saturday. Carry Phone to help you by listening to good music as you run.
- Character - Improved stamina and energy so to better display God's joy as you do His work.

Scraping the Plate:

Read 2 Timothy 2:4-6 again and examine how each of the three examples of workers has to be determined in order to accomplish their goals. Why are their goals not always easy to achieve? How did Paul go on to testify of his own determination in verses 7-10 to preach the gospel?

Sunday Roast:

Belonging to the family of God, provides the determination to work hard.

RESOURCEFULNESS - the ability to deal well with new or difficult situations and find solutions to problems; being inventive

"And God blessed them. And God said to them, 'Be fruitful and multiply and fill the earth and subdue it, and have dominion over the fish of the sea and over the birds of the heavens and over every living thing that moves on the earth'." Genesis 1:28

Scripture Text: Psalm 8

It is amazing, the creativity of men and women, boys and girls around the world. God has made us that way. He commanded from the very beginning that we subdue and have dominion over this world. Ever since Adam and Eve, people have been coming up with new inventions out of the resources around them, and creating new ways of accomplishing jobs more efficiently and quickly. Adam and Eve made clothes from fig leaves. God then gave them a better idea by making clothing from animal skins.

Besides the fact that God made trees to produce oxygen and provide shelter and shade, man has invented thousands of uses for wood and tree products: dye, piano keys, rayon, paper, fishing floats, ping pong balls, photographic film, sugar, syrup, chewing gum, diapers, medicines, waxes, cider, antacids, rubber, toothpaste, furniture, and more.

Man has also been extremely creative in the uses for the peanut including: chili sauce, oil, shampoo, shaving cream, glue, caramel, and even insecticide. Thanks to men like George

Washington Carver, who embraced his God-given role to have dominion over the earth, there have been hundreds of discoveries for peanuts, soybeans, almonds, pecans, sweet potatoes, corn, etc. From variations of food products to paints, man has produced items to make life better. Using ginger, cinnamon, and other natural spices for health benefits has been a creative idea for centuries. Creating new building resources out of recyclable products is a growing creative trend.

Solomon was a man of creativity. He made life in Israel better and safer in Israel for everyone to enjoy. He provided an armory, planted vineyards and orchards, imported apes and peacocks, invented musical instruments, and more. However, we must remember in all our creativity that, like Solomon, we are mere humans. Jesus warned in Matthew 12:42 that when we rise up in pride and refuse to recognize God as our father and Jesus as our Lord, we will be judged. God is the giver of life and gifts of men. Jesus is our enabler and Savior. Everything we do is not to be done for our own enjoyment without recognition and glory going to the One who made us and to whom we serve. George Washington Carver once said, *"I love to think of nature as an unlimited broadcasting station, through which God speaks to us every hour, if we will only tune in."*

Taste Test:

One of the ways my parents encouraged my siblings and me to be creative were by making us find our own means of entertainment. They would give us paper, buttons, string, sticks, glue, an Erector set, etc and let us create. We learned to make up our own board games, build toys, and use our imagination. This provided the fuel later in life to solve problems when there was a need.

- Set aside time with your family and you use your imagination to create. Find a project around your house or yard where you can work together to be creative.
- Set aside a Saturday where the technological devices are put aside and you teach the kids how to play using their imagination.
- Play an old board game but make up your own new rules, or create your own game.

These can produce the spirit of creativity God has provided us.

There are always ways to research and produce new and better products for life. As long as there is work to be done, disease to be conquered, or time to be saved, there will always be the need for new and creative ideas. Use your resourcefulness to create solutions.

Scraping the Plate:

Read Psalm 8 and list the ways mankind has found uses for God's creation, especially in verses 6-8. This is just a minute amount of God's creation! Pray a prayer of thanksgiving for all that God has given us and ask Him to help us be better stewards of His resources.

Sunday Roast:

God is the creator of all things, and He made us in His image. One way we display His image is in our creativity and resourcefulness. God made us to subdue and have dominion over this earth. We are to use it to better the lives of others. Let's be image-bearers for Christ by the resourceful service we provide to the community around us.

CHAPTER 4

Purpose

- Patience
- Courage
- Humility
- Resourcefulness
- Awareness
- Endurance
- Flexibility
- Joyfulness
- Love
- Responsibility
- Righteousness

PATIENCE - the state of being able to remain calm and not annoyed when waiting for a long time; maintaining a inner peace when dealing with problems or difficult people

"I waited patiently for the Lord; He inclined to me and heard my cry," Psalm 40:1

Scripture Text: Luke 2:22-35

Waiting has always been and will always be one of the most difficult things to do. When one's heart and mind are full of anticipation or longing, it is challenging to endure the time as it passes. That was the situation for Israel as they awaited the arrival of their promised Messiah. They longed for the one who was to be King in the line of David, their greatest king in history. They anticipated the Sent One because prophecy said that he would bring good news to the poor, heal the broken hearted, free the captives, deliver prisoners, comfort those in mourning, and usher in his kingdom that would have no end.

Yet, over four hundred years passed by since the last of the prophets had given those encouraging words. Not since Malachi prophesied sometime between 425-450 B.C. that the Messiah would be born in Bethlehem and be preceded by Elijah had there been a prophetic word. Day after day passed by until most of Israel forgot or gave no attention to the promises of God.

Yet, in Jerusalem, there lived an elderly man, Simeon, to whom God had given an individual promise in his heart by the Holy Spirit. The Spirit promised him that he would not see death until he had first seen the Messiah born. Simeon had not forgotten God's prophecies or promises. He was *"waiting for the consolation of Israel."* It was not an act of coincidence or luck that he happened to be in the Temple the day Mary and Joseph arrived to offer sacrifice according to the Jewish custom. The Holy Spirit was upon him, so *"he came in the Spirit into the Temple: and when the parents brought in the child Jesus, to do for him according to the custom of the law, he took him up in his arms and blessed God."*

The beauties of this story are evident both with God and Simeon:

- God never forsakes His people and always keeps His promises. God is patient with all people and is working according to His timetable, not ours, to accomplish what is best for all.
- Simeon demonstrates how we should endure during periods of waiting. He was righteous and devout and filled with the Holy Spirit.

Scripture declares that the righteous live by faith. Simeon was living every day trusting in God to fulfill His Word and care for him in the mean time. His faith in God and God's promised Messiah, like Abraham, was accounted to him for righteousness. He was devout; meaning he continued faithfully to serve and worship the Lord according to the knowledge given to him. He did not make excuses that it had been 'forever' since there had been a good message at the synagogue. He was not self-righteous in abiding by law or by outward works or gratuity. Rather, he genuinely worshiped the Lord from his heart and therefore God abided with him through His Spirit. He sought the presence of God.

Taste Test:

Practice waiting! It might be fun to be spontaneous and carefree, but it also beneficial to teach ourselves to be patient. In light of our culture, where people want everything instantaneously, patience has to be nurtured. Show your children the difference between 'fast food' and gourmet prepared meals. Explain the old adage "haste makes waste." Thank goodness, not everything takes a long time, but there are some things worth the waiting. It took Michelangelo over four years to paint the Sistine Chapel ceiling. It took the Borglums over fourteen years to carve Mt. Rushmore.

Find a project that you can do as a family together that takes time. Work on it a little at a time so that you can enjoy the process and do quality work: landscape the yard, repaint, build a playground, or write a book. The choices are endless.

Scraping the Plate:

Read Psalm 40 again, giving attention to the work of salvation described in verses 2-3.

- How does 'waiting for the Lord' fit into our trust in the Lord?
- Does verse 4 imply that if we do not wait in faith for the fulfillment of our salvation from God in Jesus, we

will probably 'trust in' or 'lean upon' false ideas that man has conceived?

- Does the psalmist ending with a plea for God not to delay His deliverance mean that he was impatient or does it demonstrate the psalmist's trust and dependence on God?
- Share your thoughts with each other.

Biscuits and Gravy:

Ability begins with effort in learning. Skill is developed over time and with continued effort. Therefore patience is a necessary quality in accomplishing the purposes of God.

COURAGE - the strength of heart to face and conquer fear or difficulties

"Be strong and courageous. Do not fear or be in dread of them: for it is the Lord your God who goes with you; He will not leave you or forsake you." Deuteronomy 31:6

Scripture Text: 1 Timothy 4:12; 2 Timothy 1:7, 3:1-4:5

It has been said that Timothy had several reasons to be afraid. To begin with Timothy was a companion to Paul and Silas on their missionary journey and witnessed the hardships and persecution they endured. First seeing Paul, as described in Acts 16, as he arrived in town, still bearing the scars and bruises from having been stoned and left for dead may have made Timothy uncomfortable. Then as Timothy traveled with Paul when Paul was beaten and thrown in prison in Philippi must have provoked some anxiety in Timothy's heart.

Also, Timothy was young. The responsibility of carrying on the work of the Lord for Paul must have been stressful. Not everyone respects a younger person trying to teach them, nor do they want them correcting them when they are wrong. Paul, however, encouraged Timothy not to let others despise his youthfulness. Paul encouraged Timothy in his letters not to be afraid. *"For God has not given us the spirit of fear; but of power, and of love, and of a sound mind."* 2 Timothy 1:7. Paul further gives Timothy a charge in the second letter to Timothy saying, *"continue in the things which you have learned and been assured of,"* and *"I charge you before God and the Lord Jesus Christ, who will judge the quick and the dead at His appearing and His kingdom, Preach the Word..."*

Timothy may have had a natural tendency to be timid, shy, reserved, or introverted, but to Paul none of that mattered in regard to the calling and work of the Lord. Paul wanted Timothy to understand two things about his natural fear. First, timidity comes from the same source as pride. Our selfish nature wants to promote itself or care for itself. An extroverted person may be arrogant and demanding of their wants, while a timid person draws into seclusion. However, both individuals do so for the same reason, they are protecting their interests in themselves, just in extremely different ways. God has warned against the pitfalls of pride and how it separates us from God's grace. All individuals, whether extroverted or shy, must learn to trust and depend on God for His provision. Secondly, Paul wanted Timothy to know that God was with him. He need not to be afraid, because God was always going to be right by his side in everything that he went through. Paul knew that first hand and wanted Timothy to find courage in that truth.

Taste Test:

What causes you to be afraid? Are you shy? Do you have other fears such as water, heights, or speaking in front of a crowd? Are you allowing these fears to keep you from serving the Lord in any way?

One of the greatest lessons I learned in life was to overcome my fears by facing them. I have always had a fear of heights, so I made myself climb a ladder to do roof work and painting. Because of that I have since been able to ride the gondola across the Royal Gorge in Colorado and do zip-line and rope-course obstacles at youth retreats. I also never learned to swim well. It seems I sink well though. However, by facing that fear of sinking rather than floating, I learned to work as a swimming pool builder and maintenance man for a few years when I was younger. I actually was able to dive into a deep pool to work on the drain without fear. I simply used a pole to help me get back to the top.

- Choose an area of your fears and examine how it might be keeping you back from serving the Lord more fully, then pray together as a family for practical ways in which you might be able to face your fears. If you fear crowds, maybe you could start by going to a shelter and helping serve food to the poor.

Scraping the Plate:

Discuss the passage in Deuteronomy 31 as to why Moses was encouraging the people and Joshua not to be afraid.

Can you think of reasons that they would fear their future? What caused the children of Israel so many problems from this time in history and forward? Did they soon forget that God was with them in such a way that He alone was their provider and God? How does God's constant presence empower us. How do Christians today have a huge blessing through the Holy Spirit?

Biscuits and Gravy:

When we have great opportunities in front of us, the courage that God provides through our relationship with Him drives us to fulfill those purposes.

HUMILITY - the quality or state of mind where one does not think of themselves as better than others; lowliness of heart; meekness of spirit

"Do nothing from selfish ambition or conceit, but in humility count others more significant than yourselves." Philippians 2:3

Scripture Text: Philippians 2:2,13; 3:12-21

There once was a young medical student who graduated top of his class in both his undergraduate work at Howard Payne College in Brownwood, Texas and his post-graduate studies. He was soon recognized at medical school by the elite team of doctors in Houston, Texas, led by the famous Dr. Michael DeBakey. Dr. DeBakey offered this young intern, Gene Burrows, a position on his surgical team. This was a position of high honor and probably would have led to a successful and lucrative career. Gene, however, graciously declined the offer as he humbly gave himself to be a medical missionary in Bangladesh. He stated his appreciation for the honor of being asked to work on such an elite team, but added that he had a higher calling to minister to the underprivileged and lost of the world. Dr. Gene Burrows never considered himself too good to serve those in the world's worst conditions. Instead he spent the next sixty plus years providing care to people in Bangladesh and the Ivory Coast. He used his medical profession as a tool and position to share the light of the gospel to those in poverty and turmoil.

The apostle Paul stated his own recognition of the fact that he had a long way to go in becoming like Jesus, his Lord. He said in Phil. 3:12, "Not as though I had already attained." Paul was a man of great education, political zeal, and work ambition. He had every reason to be proud of his accomplishments. However, he considered all of his personal ability and success meaningless in comparison to knowing Christ Jesus (Phil. 3:7-8). He cared little for the praise and honor of men. Knowing that God was preparing an eternal home and a glorious transformation for those who follow Christ. Paul encouraged believers to press on toward pleasing God, which is a theme he initiated in chapter 2. As Christ humbled Himself to please His Father, so we please God by thinking of the needs of others. That is why he stated, *"in humility count others more significant than yourself."* Phil. 2:3.

Taste Test:

Next time you are at the grocery store, try this exercise.

- Notice how many people are oblivious to those around them, or are deliberately rude to others. Some people, because of their thoughtlessness toward others, block the aisles with their carts as they stand and talk with friends. Some people rush through and cut in front of others as if they think they are more important. Many people in groups spread out as they walk down the aisles and will not move to the side to let individuals pass by.

- After you watch others behavior for poor examples, make sure that you take notice of any good examples as well. Compliment them for their humble kindness. When you are ready to check out, deliberately let someone else go in front of you to purposefully encourage him or her to also act graciously and humbly.
- When you get back to your car, share the examples of poor behavior that you saw and how it made you feel. Then share how the opportunity to let someone else go ahead of you made you feel; share what was his or her reaction.

Scraping the Plate:

Read Philippians 2:4 and define what humility is in your own words.

Humility is consideration of others above one's self. A great way to grow in humility is to notice other's needs and work to meet those needs; it may even at the expense of our own needs not being met, or before our own needs are met. We should look for opportunities to help others. Share with each other examples of people you know who display humility in their actions toward others. Contrast that with examples of arrogant people who display selfishness.

Biscuits and Gravy:

To accomplish the purposes of Christ in service, humility is essential.

RESOURCEFULNESS - "the ability to deal well with new or difficult situations and find solutions to problems; being inventive"

"Great is our Lord, and abundant in power; His understanding is beyond measure" Psalm 147:5

Scripture Text: Nehemiah 4

During December in the Austrian Alps, Father Joseph Mohr was planning the Christmas Eve service at the newly built St. Nicholas Church in Obendorf near Salzburg. The only problem was that the church's organ had been damaged, hindering the music program. Father Joseph used his imagination and resourcefulness to write the lyrics of *Tiroler Volkslied,* Tyrolean folk song, which the organist, Franz Gruber, accompanied with the guitar. The song was sung for the first time December 24th, 1818 and was a great success. By 1838 the song was a Christmas favorite all across German-speaking Europe and in 1863 the English translation took America by storm. *"Silent Night, Holy Night, All is calm, all is bright."* Father Mohr did not know his last minute resourcefulness would lead to such a classic, favorite song. Nor did he know it would become famous, but endless amounts of people are grateful to him for the song's impact on their lives.

Nehemiah had to be resourceful when faced with opposition while trying to rebuild the walls of Jerusalem. When Sanballat and Tobiah threatened the work, Nehemiah gathered the leaders together and they joined in support of a plan. They resourcefully derived a plan for the workers to take turns, some building the wall while others guarded it. They all carried their weapons by their side as they worked. The workers were provided places to stay in the city at night so that the work never stopped. What an amazing way to be resourceful in administration. Nehemiah also devised a communication system using trumpets to warn and rally each other in case of an attack. This thwarted the enemies' opposition and the walls of Jerusalem were finished in record time.

Don't be afraid of opportunities ahead of you because they are difficult or new. Be resourceful by leaning on the Lord's wisdom. He will guide you to accomplish great and mighty things beyond what you could even imagine.

Taste Test:

God is our ultimate example of inventiveness or resourcefulness, creating the entire earth and universe in only six days. Not to mention many others examples of His creativity in scripture, He has also blessed us with a creative spirit. A successful inventor's talent is quite apparent as one studies human history from the Egyptians to modern times. Athletes are always inventing new ways to improve performance in their sport; businessmen and women create new ideas to further the success of their company. One only needs a problem or challenge to incite the creative spirit within in finding a solution.

- Do you have a problem that you need to fix?
- Encourage the creative spirit in your children and family through art, music, woodwork, or some other hobby in which you can make things.

Scraping the Plate:

Spend the time as a family discussing how God demonstrates His creativity and inventiveness. Look at examples of odd creatures in the world that He has made, or discover interesting ways in which nature works, like the honeybee. Read Job 38-41 and listen as God, Himself, describes His own works to Job. Then say to the Lord with Job, *"I know that you can do everything and that no thought can be withheld from you."* Discuss how we can trust God, who is so amazing and capable, to enable us to do whatever we need to do in a time of creative necessity.

Biscuits and Gravy:

Being resourceful is a many faceted quality encompassing creativity, frugalness, flexibility, and dependence. Those who confound the wise of this world with His ways accomplish God's purposes. Let the Lord lead you into being resourceful as you serve His purposes.

AWARENESS - knowing and recognizing that something exists; finding wonder in and noticing the world around you

"By this we know love, that He laid down His life for us, and we ought to lay down our lives for the brothers. But if anyone has the world's goods and sees his brother in need, yet closes his heart against him, how does God's love abide in him? 1 John3:16-17

Scripture Text: Matthew 14:15-21, John 6:1-13

During my years in the ministry I have had the opportunity to be in many people's home and see their needs. I have traveled to poverty stricken regions and seen devastation. I met a man once dying of cancer. He still lived alone in his home because he could not afford help. His home was old and in disrepair. There were gaps in the walls and floor that the light and wind could seep through. He heated his water with a homemade electric iron-rod that he would drop into the water. He had very little furniture and was sleeping on a mattress on the floor of the kitchen because that was the only room he could afford to heat. Similar situations to this have been repeated in my ministry over and over.

I went to New Orleans after Katrina and worked with a crew to help clean the flood victims' houses. There were hundreds of homes that I saw where people were trying to rebuild their lives, yet their homes were *gutted* down to the frame and all their belongings were ruined and piled in the yard. Similarly, after a hurricane hit the coast of Texas, I visited and worked with the Texas Baptist Men in Port Lavaca. While delivering meals, I witnessed a lady sweeping her kitchen floor, yet she had no walls or ceiling around her. I previously ministered at the Star of Hope Mission in central Houston. Hundreds of homeless men and women would gather at night for a warm meal and a bed in which to sleep.

What I have seen is minute in comparison to the millions in the world that are underprivileged and starving. When Jesus saw the multitudes he was moved to compassion. It amazes me that the disciples saw the same people, yet wanted to send them away. They questioned their ability to help so apparently planned to do nothing. Jesus taught his disciples that it is our responsibility to be aware of the needs of others and to reach out to them in their need. We might not be sufficient to meet their need, but we know someone who is - Jesus Christ. Matthew 14:18 is a great verse to memorize, *"He said, 'Bring them here to me.'"* John remembered this when he wrote his letters to the churches. He reminded the early believers that we, as Christ-followers, must demonstrate Christ's love by giving and ministering to the needs of those around us. If we shut our eyes to their needs, while having the ability to help, the love of God is not truly in us.

Jesus came with that purpose in mind both physically and spiritually. He said, *"The Spirit of the Lord in upon me, because He has anointed me to preach the gospel to the poor; He has sent me to heal the brokenhearted, to preach deliverance to the captives, and recovering of sight to the blind, to set at liberty those that are bruised,"* in Luke 4:18. Are you aware of the hurting around you and are you following the Lord's example? It has been said that if you need more faith - read God's Word. If you need more power - pray. If you need more compassion - go. Maybe we just need to get out where we will see the needs around us so that God can instill His heart for others into our chest." *A new heart also will I give you, and a new spirit will I put within you: and I will take away the stony heart out of your flesh, and I will give you a heart of flesh."* Ezekiel 36:26

Taste Test:

In order to be aware of people's needs we have to see what they are experiencing. You have to plan to be involved based on your ability and availability.

- One way to start is take a drive in your area and pray that God will open your eyes to be aware of possible needs.
- Then, find a local mission to visit; inquire about a food distribution ministry in your area.
- Ask pastors in your area about ministries to the poor, homeless, sick, or imprisoned.
- Let God lead you into a ministry project that can be your hands and feet of Jesus.

Scraping the Plate:

Read Micah, chapter 2. In this passage, as well as several other Old Testament prophetic warnings, God's people are warned of judgment because they did not practice hospitality and compassion. Rather, the people lived in materialism, comfort brought about by greed and covetousness, and a false sense of religious hypocrisy. Discuss how we, as God's children, should balance respect for God's blessings and the use of His provision, with accountability to give and meet the needs of others. Are we storing up more, in this life of earthly goods and wealth, than we are laying up treasures in Heaven through our good works?

Biscuits and Gravy:

Being aware of the truth of the gospel, that God loves, cares, and provides the hope of salvation for all individuals gives purpose to our life of service. We have the greatest resource to offer those in need - Jesus.

ENDURANCE - the ability to do something difficult for a long time, or put up with pain and suffering that continues for a period of time

"...and let us run with endurance the race that is set before us." Hebrews 12:1b

Scripture Text: Hebrews 11:35-38

John Bunyan, the famous English preacher and writer of *Pilgrim's Progress,* spent twelve years in prison for preaching the gospel and refusing to conform to the state religion that denied salvation by grace. The Auca Indians of Ecuador, whom he was trying to reach with the gospel, murdered Elizabeth Elliot's husband. Elizabeth then spent two years living among the Auca Indians herself. The very men who killed her husband became her friends and new brothers in Christ as she taught them of God's love and forgiveness. David Brainerd, missionary to Native American Indians, endured persecution from hypocritical religious hierarchy during college and was expelled. He later continued to endure difficulties while trying to minister to the Indians of New England as he was suffering from tuberculosis.

Each of these individuals endured hardships for the sake of serving the Lord through their service to share the gospel. It was extremely difficult for John Bunyan because his wife and children were dependent upon the generosity of friends and church members for their survival. John tried to earn money to help them through his writing, but they were extremely poor. John counted this experience as a necessity. He stated that he could not compromise the truth of the gospel and that if he must suffer for the sake of preaching the truth, then he would. David Brainerd died of tuberculosis at the age of 29. He only served on the mission field for about six years, but during that time he endured loneliness, hunger, cold, and the ridicule of religious leaders from Yale University. Many times he felt so bad from these difficulties that he would fall into a state of depression. Elizabeth Elliot's story is one of the most intriguing. Enduring the loss of her husband, who was murdered simply trying to deliver gifts to the Auca Indians, Elizabeth faced fear and danger by going to minister to those very murderers.

What did these great Christian heroes' endurance produce? *Pilgrim's Progress* became the second best-selling book, only surpassed by the Bible, ever to be published. Its message has inspired millions in their Christian walk. An entire tribe of people in Ecuador came to know the Lord and establish a church. The Delaware Indians established the first Native American Christian community with a membership of over 130 people.

Hebrews 11:35-38 talks about believers who had an amazing ability to endure difficulties and accomplish great things. These early believers suffered and endured torture, imprisonment, mockery, and even death for the sake of sharing the gospel and God's love with those who did not yet believe. Their desire was to shine as a beacon of God's grace and love so that some would trust in Jesus as their Savior. Endurance for the spreading of the gospel has been a trademark of the Christian church. It is easy to endure difficulties for those you love and love you. It is another thing entirely to endure suffering at the hand of those who hate you while loving them enough to share the gospel with them. God has a special reward, however, for those who endure.

Taste Test:

Developing a desire to spread the gospel without fear is important for every believer.

- Ask your pastor if he has opportunities within your church where you could share your testimony. This is a safe place to begin.
- Write out your testimony of how you became a Christian including scripture that explains how to trust the Lord as Savior. Including scripture like the "Roman Road" passages is a great way to share the gospel truth.
- Then print out your testimony on a piece of paper. Carry copies with you when you go out to eat, or shopping. Simply ask the waitress or clerk if you could give them a copy of your personal testimony. You will be surprised at how easy it becomes. If you put your church's phone number and address on the bottom of your testimony, you might see some of these individuals respond.

Scraping the Plate:

One of the greatest ways to encourage one's faith is reading the biographies of past Christians. Find a biography of David Brainerd, Jim and Elizabeth Elliot, John Bunyan, or others like

Amy Carmichael and Eric Liddell. Discuss how they demonstrated great endurance and how that endurance was worth it for the kingdom of God.

Biscuits and Gravy:

Sharing the gospel and serving the Lord may require a lot of endurance, but knowing we are accomplishing the eternal purpose of God makes it a joy.

FLEXIBILITY - the state of being able to easily change or adjust; ability to do different things, adapt to new and different or challenging requirements

"Many times he delivered them, but they were rebellious in their purposes and were brought low through their iniquity. Nevertheless, he looked upon their distress, when he heard their cry. For their sake he remembered his covenant and relented according to the abundance of his steadfast love. He caused them to be pitied by all those who held them captive." Psalm 106: 43-46

Scripture Text: John 2:1-12, Matthew 8 & 9, Mark 1

It is easy to point out the love of Jesus or His obedience, courage, kindness, and hospitality, but with a little observation we can also see how flexible Jesus was. Jesus seemed to adjust his schedule or time for the benefit of others to show the love of God. Chapter 2 of the gospel of John tells the story of how Jesus turned the water into wine. Even though it was not time to reveal himself as the Messiah, Jesus honored His mother and adjusted His plans to meet the needs of those present. This was not something that He apparently planned to do, but He did so, in part, to help a friend. This act was also done to encourage the faith of His disciples.

Matthew 8:5-13 unveils the story of Jesus healing the servant of a centurion. This was an interruption in His schedule, but He adjusted. In Matthew 9:23-26, Jesus follows a ruler back to his house to raise his daughter from the dead. Along the way a woman touches the hem of His garment and Jesus is flexible enough to stop and bless her for her faith. Mark 1:30-31 tells of Jesus healing Peter's mother-in-law. This again was not planned, but she was in need and He adjusted His plans to meet that need.

Jesus was always willing to change His schedule for the sake of caring and serving other peoples' needs. It seems as if every miracle was an interruption in His scheduled routine. We too should be flexible to adjust our schedule and not be irritated or dismayed when an opportunity to serve others arises.

Taste Test:

This week while running errands, heading to and from classes, or going about your daily routine, try to keep your eyes open for people who could use a helping hand. You might be surprised how many times an opportunity presents itself.

Scraping the Plate:

Being flexible is not about planning to help someone in a time of need, as wonderful and great an idea as that is. Being flexible is about being available in the spur of the moment, even when it is inconvenient. Gong out of your way to help a friend or stranger, much like the Good Samaritan, is a great way to demonstrate the love of God. Discuss the passage in Psalm 106 where the psalmist is rehearsing God's mercy to the children of Israel. Can you see the flexibility of God and His mercy when He could have poured out judgment?

Biscuits and Gravy:

Serving the Lord means that we are not living to serve ourselves, therefore we must be flexible to accomplish His purposes when an opportunity arises.

JOYFULNESS - the feeling of great happiness or delight evoked by inner wellbeing, success, or good fortune

"You will show me the path of life, in your presence is fullness of joy; at your right hand there are pleasures *forevermore."* Psalm 16:11

Scripture Text: 1 Thessalonians 2:19-20

Joy does not only have to be the by-product of one's own wellbeing, success, or good fortune. It can also be the joy in seeing others succeed and be blessed. I am reminded that Jesus taught us to be good neighbors. A good neighbor is a person who ministers to the needs of anyone with whom he comes in contact. In Matthew 25:35-40, Jesus also taught that as we serve to meet the needs of others, we do it unto Him. There is a great connection between the heart of the person serving willingly and those being served.

Paul's first letter to the Thessalonian believers, written while he was imprisoned in Rome, illustrates the connection of care. Paul deeply cared for the believers in Thessalonica because it was one of the first places he visited in that part of the world and he helped begin the church there. As he cared for and encouraged these believers, they, in turn, ministered to him in his time of need.

In Paul's letter he had a very particular thought in mind about how and where joy was appropriated. He says, *"are not even you in the presence of our Lord Jesus Christ at His coming?"* Paul had grown through life's trials and difficulties to understand that the place of greatest joy is in the presence of God. He knew that the Lord Jesus, by being at the right hand of the Father, was the source of the *fullness of joy* and *pleasures forevermore.* Paul's delight and joy was knowing that these friends, believers in Christ, in Thessalonica and surrounding areas walked in the presence of the Lord Jesus Christ. Even though Paul could not be with them, Jesus was. Also being aware that when Jesus returns, we will all be together with Him. Paul wanted these believers, who had brought joy to him through their care, to know the deep joy he had in Jesus.

Taste Test:

Romans 12:15 encourages us to rejoice with others when they have reason to rejoice, and weep with those who have reason to be sad. Many times we focus only on our own problems and successes. We are quick to want everyone to listen to our good news, and jealous when others have good news. We want others to hear our sad stories of need, but listen to others with judgment.

- Plan to carry a notepad and jot down other people's life stories.
- Send a card of encouragement to those hurting and a card of congratulations to those celebrating.
- Call or meet with a friend to offer encouragement or congratulations.

Scraping the Plate:

Read Acts 16:9 - 17:9 and make note of all the reasons Paul and Silas had to rejoice. Compare that to the difficulties they faced. Discuss how the encounters with Lydia, the Philippian jailer, and the Thessalonians were more important to Paul because they caused eternal relationship and joys whereas the difficulties were only temporary.

Biscuits and Gravy:

Scripture states the desire accomplished is sweet to the soul. There is no greater joy than in serving the Lord's purpose of leading others to Him.

LOVE - a feeling of strong affection as in romance, attraction, and devotion to another person or thing

"And hope does not put us to shame, because God's love has been poured out into our hearts through the Holy Spirit who has been given to us." Romans 5:5

Scripture Text: Genesis 45:1-5

One of the goals we had in the Baker home when our children were growing up, was for our children to truly be friends as well as siblings. We nurtured love in them by encouraging respect for each other, appreciation for each other's differences, not condoning fighting or rudeness to each other, guiding them in forgiveness and genuine repentance. Home is the first place children learn to love. Love is both taught and caught. We had to demonstrate love by our own forgiveness and repentance. We had to show them respect and acceptance by practicing these in our marriage. But, more than from us, love is caught from a relationship with God, through His Holy Spirit.

In Romans 5:5 Paul writes that love is poured out into our hearts. The Greek word for 'poured out' is *ekcheo,* which portrays the meaning 'to gush or to spill out or upon.' It gives the description of abundance and dispersion. Our desire should be for our children to have an abundant desire to care for each other, spend time together, and enjoy each other. Love cannot be performed under restraint or demand; it must proceed from the heart.

The story of Joseph is an excellent picture of this lesson. Love may not have been displayed well in Jacob's home since Jacob showed favoritism toward Rachel's children over Leah's and their handmaids'. Joseph had caught the love of God, as scripture so beautifully demonstrates when Joseph revealed himself to his brothers in Egypt. Remember these brothers had despised Joseph because of the favoritism of their father and the dreams that God had given him.

Joseph spent years in an Egyptian prison unjustly as a result of their abandonment. Yet, when his brothers came to Egypt and the time was right, Joseph revealed himself to them. Great waves of emotion, that Joseph could not contain, swept over him. He wanted to have time with his brothers to comfort and encourage them. Beginning with Benjamin, he threw his arms around them all and wept. What Joseph felt was the confirmation of the Holy Spirit's guidance and love being poured out through him. The way he loved was in agreement with the way scripture describes God's love. "*Bearing with one another and, if one has a complaint against another, forgiving each other; as the Lord has forgiven you, so you also must forgive. And above all these things put on love, which binds everything together in perfect harmony,*" Colossians 3:13-14.

Whether we were teaching our children love through discipline and example, or leading them in their relationship with God that they might catch His love through the Holy Spirit, our desire was that they would be sincere. "*Let love be genuine. Abhor what is evil; hold fast to what is good. Love one another with brotherly affection.*" Romans 12:9-10.

Taste Test:

All children fight because of the nature of selfishness within them, whether it is boys wrestling when they get upset or girls bickering over displeasures. How parents use that to provide instruction and guidance is crucial.

- Rather than wait until the next time, gather your family together and discuss how they usually behave when they get upset with each other.
- Role-play a scene for them (or let them act it out) of their behavior, and then ask them to role-play how God would prefer them to respond.
- Provide time and opportunity for confession and repentance if this is necessary.

Scraping the Plate:

Read John 13:34-35 and Galatians 5:13. How do these verses teach us that our behavior is a type of witness and testimony before the lost world? Would others want to be a Christian if they watched you and your siblings together?

Biscuits and Gravy:

Because love is not always easy to bestow on those who are unlovely in actions and character, love must be motivated in these cases by the purpose of God. The greatest way to lose an enemy is to make him a friend. That is exactly how God wooed us to salvation, *"But God demonstrated His love to us...when we were enemies we were reconciled to God."*
Romans 5:8-10

RESPONSIBILITY - a duty or task that you are required or expected to do; the state of being accountable for what you are expected or have committed to accomplish

" *Man goes out to his work and to his labor until the evening."* Psalm 104:23 "*The desire of the sluggard kills him, for his hands refuse to labor."* Proverbs 21:25

Scripture Text: Acts 18:1-3, 2 Thessalonians 3:7-9

From the time I was young, I worked. My parents believed their children needed to learn the responsibility of keeping up with their own possessions, caring for things around them, and working to earn money. I was given chores to clean my room, pick up my toys, help with the house cleaning, do the laundry, wash dishes, feed animals, mow the yard, and more. I began working to earn my own money when I was about twelve. I mowed neighbors' yards and worked in my family's pet store. Growing up, my family was not rich, nor did we have many possessions. My parents never owned a home or a new vehicle. We rented and bought items used. This upbringing, however, taught me to value the things that God had blessed me with and to not cherish material possessions inappropriately. Also, it taught me the value of working responsibly. There are few greater joys than working to accomplish something or build something and seeing it through to the end. "*The desire accomplished is sweet to the soul,*" Proverbs 13:19.

The apostle Paul is a great example of working responsibly. When he traveled across the country establishing churches for God, he could have leaned on the new believers to take care of him. Rather than put that burden on young Christians who were still learning how to follow Jesus, Paul worked as a tentmaker to support himself. He wanted to set an example to these new believers on Christian character. He wanted these new Christ-followers to work with integrity and honesty. He, therefore, lived in front of them the way he wanted them to live in the world around them. That sometimes caused conflict when people were being dishonest or abusive, and Paul spoke out against it like he did in Philippi. There a group of men were using a young maiden as a fortune-teller and getting rich off of her ability. They told people that certain Greek gods had given her this talent. Then they sold trinkets and souvenirs to travelers. Paul exposed this as being both dishonest and lazy. Paul later told the Thessalonian believers that, "*if any would not work, neither should he eat.*" To Paul, work was an honorable and a privileged responsibility.

Taste Test:

Do you have chores within your home?

- Make a list of the responsibilities each person should carry based upon their age and ability.
- Recognize those who do their chores well and with a good attitude.
- If your children are old enough, help them find a job where they can earn their own money.

Scraping the Plate:

Read 2 Thessalonians 3:6-12 and discuss Paul's encouragement to the Christians in this church regarding work. In colonial America, English Captain John Smith used this passage in dealing with the 'Gentlemen' or wealthy explorers who settled at Jamestown, Virginia. When they were lazy and refused to work because they only wanted to search for gold, Smith had to reprimand them. Take a moment to look up that story and read the problems they faced because of laziness. Discuss the value of hard work.

Biscuits and Gravy:

Work is a way of life and a joy to those who embrace it. Solomon said labor is a gift from God. The responsibility of labor provides purposeful motivation that gives value to a person's spirit.

RIGHTEOUSNESS - the quality of being morally good and obedient to religious laws and divine ethics; free from guilt or sin

"The mouth of the righteous speaks wisdom, and his tongue talk of justice," Psalm 37:30

Scripture Text: Luke 23:32-43, Matthew 27:44

Scripture declares that what comes out of the mouth proceeds from the heart in Matthew 15:18. So if a person has been made righteous before God through their saving relationship with Jesus Christ, their conversation ought to show it.

This can be best understood when one looks closely at the account of the two criminals who hung on either side of Jesus at Calvary. As the story unfolds, Jesus has been condemned, beaten, and led to Calvary to be crucified. Two criminals are taken along who have also been condemned to die. The crowds of people are vile and malicious. Incited by the religious leaders, they cast insults and mockery at the perfect Son of God. Amazingly, even as they are nailed to their crosses, both the criminals join in to belittle and mock Jesus as well.

Jesus' righteousness can be seen by what came out of his mouth during this horrible and glorious event. *"Father, forgive them for they do not know what they are doing."* Jesus later added, *"Father, into your hands I commend my spirit."* Here we see a heart of forgiveness and submission to authority. As an innocent man, He had every right to scream out for justice. To answer his mockers with an accusation of their own sins would have been understandable. Jesus did neither. He surrendered in obedience to His Father's will and took all our shame and punishment. He bore our burden on Calvary, and as the prophet Isaiah depicted, *"as a sheep before its shearers is silent, so he opened not his mouth."*

Somewhere during the events of Jesus' time of the cross, one thief changed his tune. While the first continued to revile Jesus according to verse 39 of Luke 23, the other thief rebuked the first. Verses 41-42 reveal that he made the necessary changes of heart to become a believer. He admitted his own sinfulness and repented. He acknowledged Jesus as Lord and Savior. The change in what came out of this thief's mouth over a short period of time exposes a profound transformation. *"Lord, remember me when you come into your kingdom."*

Our conversation ought to expose the righteous relationship we have with the father through Jesus. James and Peter both encourage good language that honors God in their epistles. *"Let your speech always be gracious, seasoned with salt, so that you may know how you ought to answer each person,"* is the way Paul taught. Does your language display the righteous standing of Christ in your heart?

Taste Test:

Using crude curse words, foolish jesting, and gossip; swearing careless oaths; complaining; and taking God's name in vain are all forms of language that God condemns. To help change these habits in your family, if necessary, serve as each other's accountability partners. Choose an appropriate punishment for using language that is not pleasing to the Lord. (A chore that has to be done for the day or week, a writing assignment, the giving of sincere compliments) Anytime a family member is caught he or she should be held accountable to the group and made to perform the punishment required. Continue this for a long enough period, like month, to establish a good habit of godly conversation.

Scraping the Plate:

Read Proverbs 25:11, 1 Peter 3:10, and James 1:26. Since Jesus is known as the Word of God, he expresses in everything he did on earth and continues to do in Heaven the nature of His Father. How does our language express our faith? Why do you feel that God is so concerned about our conversation? Can words hurt and/or heal?

Biscuits and Gravy:

We grow to understand that our righteousness, which is a free gift through Jesus Christ, carries with it the responsibility of serving God. We have a purpose in the ministry of reconciliation to speak the truth to the lost. Therefore our conversation ought to be righteous in content and context.

CHAPTER 5

Competence

- Resourcefulness
- Responsibility
- Availability
- Determination
- Flexibility
- Kindness
- Honesty
- Hospitality
- Loyalty

RESOURCEFULNESS - the ability to deal well with new or difficult situations and find solutions to problems; being inventive

"The prudent sees danger and hides himself, but the simple go on and suffer for it. The reward for humility and fear of the Lord is riches and honor and life." Proverbs 22:3-4

Scripture Text: 2 Kings 3

God in His great wisdom has given us the ability to use our knowledge to solve difficult situations and to find solutions. I was never taught as a boy how to work on my own vehicle or do simple repairs around the house. So after I was married and living in the Houston area, I had to rely on friends to teach me these life skills. Over time and with the help of many friends, I learned to do simple vehicle repairs. I replaced the oil, changed batteries, installed new starters and water pumps. Eventually I was able to drop an entire motor into an old '77 Chevy pick-up. How? I had two teenage neighbor boys who loved to work on cars, and I had a seasoned friend who had tons of tools and advice. Through their guidance, I learned. I even was able to use my own resourcefulness to build a tool to pull a steering column. The Bible is full of examples of individuals who had to be resourceful in a difficult times.

2 Kings 3 tells of King Jehoram of Israel, King Jehoshaphat of Judah, and the king of Edom who were faced with a battle against the Moabites. Moab had rebelled against Israel and the kings of Israel, Judah, and Edom had made an alliance to fight together. As they traveled and prepared for the battle they ran

out of water along the way. They were a week's journey into the wilderness of Edom. King Jehoram did not trust in the true and living God anymore, so he became despaired. He blamed the Lord for their difficult situation. King Jehoshaphat, however, was resourceful enough to ask for a prophet of God who would pray and seek God's guidance. The prophet Elisha was summoned. Elisha told the two kings to dig ditches in the desert wilderness' dry creek bed and that God would fill them with water. The following morning, just as the prophet had spoken, God caused a flash flood from the region of Edom to fill the valley. God used this to refresh the armies of Israel, Judah, and Edom, but He also performed this as a miracle in their deliverance. As the armies of Moab heard that they were being attacked, they rose to go to war against Israel and her allies. When Moab saw the water, it appeared to be blood to them and they assumed the armies of Israel, Judah, and Edom had not been able to get along; they must have fought and destroyed each other. Moab went down to gather the spoils of the battle only to be defeated themselves.

There are several examples of resourcefulness in this story. God, of course, is amazing in His ability to confound our understanding by what He causes. He caused the waters to rise in the ditches and creek bed to provide nourishment to the armies of Israel, Judah, and Edom. He also used the red reflection on the water to cause confusion to Moab and bring about the victory that these armies sought. Jehoshaphat was resourceful in seeking help and calling Elisha. Sometimes the greatest means of resourcefulness is asking for help.

It has been said that networking and learning from the wisdom of others is a mark of great success. Thomas A. Watson was a carpenter and machinist, yet that is who Alexander Graham Bell used as his assistant to create the telephone. Counting on others can be helpful, but never know if you don't ask.

Taste Test:

Can you think of difficult situations or problems that you and your family may be facing? Do you have something to be fixed around the house? Maybe your church needs to be resourceful if its ministry is declining.

Follow the guide of Jehoshaphat and first seek God's guidance in prayer or seek the wisdom of God's minister. Also, seek the wisdom of others by researching ideas of others who have faced similar situations. Whether your problem is fixing a broken pipe on the hot water heater or rebuilding a struggling youth ministry, God provides the resources if we will be resourceful in seeking help.

Scraping the Plate:

Read John 6:1-13. Discuss Jesus' resourcefulness to feed the 5000 men along with the women and children. Notice Jesus did not want anything to go to waste. What did he say in verse 12? Why do you think Jesus wanted to save the leftovers? Was this resourceful as well?

Pancakes:

We are enabled by God's wisdom to be resourceful. Resourceful people then are competent like their Father in heaven.

RESPONSIBILITY - a duty or task that you are required or expected to do; the state of being accountable for what you are expected or have committed to accomplish

"You shall be careful to do what has passed your lips, for you have voluntarily vowed to the Lord your God what you have promised with your mouth." Deut. 23:23

"From the fruit of his mouth a man is satisfied with good, and the work of a man's hand comes back to him." Prov. 12:14

Scripture Text: John 2:1-11

One day Jesus attended a wedding in the small town of Cana, close to the Sea of Galilee. Jesus' own mother, Mary, was serving as a hostess. The bride and groom were possibly close friends of Jesus' family. As Jesus mingled with the other guests, His mother caught Him by surprise. She told Him that the wedding party was running out of wine and asked Him to fix the problem. Mary knew that her son was responsible enough to do what was expected to help others in a difficult situation. She also knew that He would do whatever He said He would do. So she told the servants to, *"Do whatever He tells you."* Jesus was seemingly caught in an awkward position. He told Mary it was not yet time for Him, referring to the revelation of His glory as God's Son.

Should He obey His Heavenly Father or honor His earthly mother. It is amazing that Jesus always did what His Heavenly Father taught Him. He was obedient and trustworthy. He did not disobey His Father in Heaven by doing what Mary asked;

rather He obeyed God's command to honor His mother. Jesus told the servants to fill several large jars with water. When they were all filled to the brim, Jesus commanded the servants to dip some out and serve the master of the feast. To everyone's surprise and delight, the water had turned into the freshest wine that they had served all evening.

Jesus was responsible by keeping His word to obey His Heavenly Father and by being accountable to do what was necessary in a situation of need. Being responsible is keeping one's word, which Jesus always did, but it is also doing those things within our capability to help others in need. No one was ever more responsible to care for others than Jesus. *"Surely he has borne our griefs and carried our sorrows."* Isaiah 53:4.

Taste Test:

Make a responsibility card contract.

- On the card state your promise to do something for someone else.
- Record the date on which you make the promise and sign it.
- Post this card on your refrigerator or somewhere easily visible until each family member has fulfilled their word by being responsible to accomplish what they promised.

Some suggestions may be for parents to help students with school projects or subjects with which they are struggling. Children might promise to help with certain chores around the house. Families might promise to do a group project for a neighbor in need.

Scraping the Plate:

Reread John 2:5 Discuss what Mary might have thought when she asked Jesus to produce wine? What do you think Jesus meant by, "My hour has not yet come."?

Being a responsible person means that you are willing to do what you say you will do. Jesus did. Compare this story with Jesus' words in John 8:28. Notice Jesus was always obedient to do His Father's will and keep His words. Think of an instance when you took the responsibility to help someone that you promised you would.

Pancakes:

Competency is necessary to responsibility. Someone who does not strive to do his or her best is not being responsible. We would be undone for all eternity had God not given His best, because salvation required a perfect sacrifice. We should do everything we do as unto the Lord, giving Him our best effort.

AVAILABILITY - the quality or state of being ready and accessible to others or in a situation

"As for the rich in this present age, charge them not to be haughty, nor to set their hopes on the uncertainty of riches, but on God, who richly provides us with everything to enjoy. They are to do good, to be rich in good works, to be generous and ready to share, thus storing up treasure for themselves as a good foundation for the future, so that they may take hold of that which is truly life." 1 Timothy 6:17-19

Scripture Text: Judges 6:6- 7:23

Many people never get busy serving the Lord because they do not think they have anything to offer. Some of those believe a lie from Satan and do not consider how gifted they truly are. They compare their possessions and abilities with others and do not regard what they possess as a gift from God to let Him develop and use through them. Like the proverbial one talent individual, they bury their talent for fear of losing it. Paul encouraged Timothy to teach others to be ready to use their abilities to help others. One way of investing in Heaven is being *generous and ready to share.*

The act of being available for God to use us may seem scary at first. Gideon was an individual who was not looking to be available. When we first find him in Judges 6 he is hiding trying to thresh wheat for his family to make bread. Israel was being oppressed and terrorized by the Midianites. As Gideon viewed their situation, he questioned God's compassion and faithfulness rather than taking inventory of Israel's own disobedience. God reminded Gideon that He is available to His people and He will deliver them.

Then God led Gideon on an adventure like none other. Gideon, through a process of elimination, gathered together three hundred men armed with instruments seemingly unfit for battle: trumpets, torches, and clay pitchers. Through these simple tools God proved his ability to deliver His people, as they were obedient and available to serve.

God loves to confound the wise by using the simple. He chooses to use weak things to confound the strong. Our great abilities many times are only used to bring ourselves glory. But God is the only one who truly deserves glory; He loves to use people who are humble enough to be available even if they feel uncomfortable in their adequacy. God is our enabler, "*I can do all things through Christ who strengthens me.*" Philippians 4:13

Gideon told his three hundred, "*Look at me and do likewise, When I come to the outskirts of the camp, do as I do. When I blow the trumpets, I and all who are with me, then blow the trumpets also on every side of all the camp and shout, 'For the Lord and for Gideon.'*" The seemingly inferior army did as Gideon instructed. They blew the trumpets, smashed the pitchers, and held up their torches. Wow! Pitchers, trumpets, and torches were the tools God used to defeat an iron clad, sword-carrying army that had previously caused Israel to quiver while they farmed.

You may have talents and abilities that you think are unfit to serve the Lord. God says to let Him be the judge of that. He may take your availability and the talents that you make available to Him to conquer the works of Satan in your community. The encounter that Gideon had with God beside the winepress where he was hiding (Judges 6:11-24), gave him the courage to be available. Maybe you need to see God afresh and seek Him in His majesty. It was the fear and awe of God's presence that motivated Gideon to worship and serve. Truly when we know God is with us, we have nothing else to fear.

"The angel of the Lord encamps around those who fear Him, and delivers them. O fear the Lord, you his saints, for those who fear Him have no lack." Psalm 34 7,9

Taste Test:

Volunteer! Find an event where you can assist in some way. Maybe by volunteering at a civic event or in your church nursery, you can find your niche. However, you will never find it if you are not available. If you are not sure of what to do, ask others around you what they think you might be good at doing or what they do to serve.

Scraping the Plate:

Discuss many of the heroes in scripture that used what God had given them:

- Noah's ability to build, Moses' staff, Joseph's dreams, Esther's beauty, David's singing, Peter's ability to fish, Paul's zeal for Israel and knowledge of the law, Barnabas' wealth.
- Would God have accomplished His work through them if they had not used their talents and been available? What do you have? What can you do?

Pancakes:

God has gifted and enriched us with talents that only can bring Him glory if we make them available. We must first be available to serve Him with all our hearts. Never underestimate how God can use you.

DETERMINATION - the quality that makes you continue trying to do or achieve something that is difficult

"No one who puts his hand to the plow and looks back is fit for the kingdom of God." Luke 9:62

Scripture Text: Luke 9:57-62; Luke 10:1-3

One of the great heroes of the Christian faith and missionary work of the 20th century is Charles T. Studd. The Studd family was extremely wealthy and Charles was an excellent athlete. He was known all over England as one of the country's greatest cricket players. Yet, his was not a Christian home. Charles' father was saved late in life but immediately began trying to live for Jesus by witnessing to his three grown sons and hosting gospel meetings in his house. None of this moved Charles at that time, but later when his brother became deathly ill, Charles remembered his father's words and gave his life completely to the Lord. Charles demonstrated this change by his determination to follow Christ to the ends of the world at all costs.

Charles convinced six friends to join him and they went to China to work alongside Hudson Taylor. These seven together were known as the "Cambridge Seven" and their determination made national news in England. Charles worked for years in China until his health began to fail. He had to return to England temporarily, but that did not deter him. He persisted in following in the Lord's work. When his father passed away leaving him a wealthy inheritance, he continued without distraction. He gave most of his inheritance away to various

Christian leaders such as D. L. Moody and George Muller. When he recovered he returned to his missionary work for a time in south India. Later, he started a new work blazing a trail of missionary endeavors into Africa. There he created a mission work named the World-Wide Evangelization Crusade. It was on this mission field in Africa that Charles and his wife, Pricilla, both died.

The sacrifice and determination of C. T. Studd provides a great example of Jesus' words in Luke 9:62. One cannot be half-hearted in choosing to become a Christian, you either accept Jesus as Lord and Savior, or you do not. The same is true in our influence as His servants. If we are not wholly following Christ, then our work is not fit for God's kingdom and our half-heartedness may turn more away from the truth than it will ever draw to Christ.

Taste Test:

It has been said that a person's devotion can be judged by where and how they spend their time and money.

- As a family or individually, make a financial pie chart using these categories: Groceries and Utilities, Education, Home and Vehicle, Entertainment, Clothing, Church and God's service, and Savings.
- Make a similar Time Pie Chart and list categories for the different things and activities that fill your time weekly.

- After completing these two charts, evaluate how much of your resources are used to honor God and how much is for personal pleasure or gain.
- Are there ways in which you should consider restructuring your life?

Scraping the Plate:

Finish reading Luke 10:17-20 and discuss the blessing the disciples experienced for following the Lord in His work wholeheartedly. Share experiences of your own in which God has blessed you for your service, or invite your pastor to dinner and ask him to share his testimony of God's service.

Pancakes:

Serving the Lord successfully takes determination, and that commitment to Him is the fuel that the Holy Spirit uses to make us competent is His work.

FLEXIBILITY - the state of being able to easily change or adjust; ability to do different things, adapt to new and different or challenging requirements

"But I say to you who hear, Love your enemies, do good to those who hate you." "But love your enemies, and do good, and lend, expecting nothing in return, and your reward will be great, and you will be sons of the Most High, for he is kind to the ungrateful and evil. Be merciful, even as your Father is Merciful." Luke 6:27, 35-36

Scripture Text: Acts 10:10 -48

One of the most amazing creatures I ever observed was a small fish my older brother, Gary, sold in his pet store. The Archer-fish is a small brackish water fish from the waters around India, Australia, and the Philippines. What makes this little 3-4 inch creature so amazing is its ability to spit water into the air to catch its prey. It can spit a stream of water to knock down flies or other flying insects. But it is not just the method of spitting water to catch its dinner that is so odd. It is the ability to overcome the natural distortion of vision when looking from under the water to above the water. Yet even with the distorted view the Archer is able to adjust its aim. God gave this creature incredible flexibility, as it has to aim slightly off target to hit its target. This fish uses a great deal of adjustment to hit its target.

Peter, the apostle, was forced by the Holy Spirit of God to be flexible in his Jewish beliefs. One day Peter was given a dream with instructions to rise, kill, and eat. But the dream contained things to eat that were not kosher in Jewish dietary rules. God gave him this dream as a larger challenge to lead him toward receiving Gentiles into the early church. God then sent Cornelius to call Peter requesting his presence. When Peter visited Cornelius' home, the Holy Spirit anointed those believers in the same way the believers at Pentecost had been filled with the Spirit. This caused Peter to adapt his theology and recognize that God was willing to save all people of every race and gender by faith in Jesus Christ. It is important that we be flexible in our relationship with God and others as we trust and follow God's guidance.

Taste Test:

Being accepting of others when their culture and lifestyle is different than ours is not always easy, especially when it conflicts with Biblical truth. We cannot be flexible on things like the truth of the gospel. Flexibility is not a compromise of God's truth; rather, it is an appreciation of different aspects in cultures - like their food or music.

Plan a cross cultural evening where you experience a different culture and learn its history, taste its cuisine, and listen to some of its music.

Then read how the gospel is being advanced to those peoples.

Scraping the Plate:

Read Acts 10. Compare verses 28 with 34-43. Discuss when and how we are to be flexible and in what ways we should never to compromise.

Pancakes:

Following the Holy Spirit to accomplish God's work requires a flexible and obedient faith. We may never know why or how God leads the way He does, but God honors those who humbly obey.

KINDNESS - "the quality or state of being affectionate, gentle, and helpful to others; the act of wanting to and enjoying to do good deeds to make others happy"

"But if anyone has this world's goods, and sees this brother in need, yet closes his heart against him, how does God's love abide in him? Little children, let us not love in word or talk but in deed and in truth." 1 John 3:17-18

Scripture Text: Genesis 24:1-28

There are many lessons we can learn in the story of Abraham's servant seeking a bride for Isaac and finding Rebekah in Genesis 24. Abraham wanted a bride for Isaac who was not an idol worshipper, but one who knew the true and living God, teaching us to separate ourselves from the world when we marry or make covenant relationships. God providentially led the servant exactly where he should go, teaching us God's faithful guidance. However, there is an outstanding character trait that shines forth in this passage - kindness.

Abraham was getting much older and was concerned for his son's well being. Isaac had just lost his mother recently and would be alone after Abraham passed away. Abraham could not travel well so he asked his servant to travel far north to Haran and seek a bride for Isaac, from among his cousins there. Fathers arranged the marriages of their children in those days and in the Middle Eastern culture. The servant was kind enough to agree. He travelled the long distance from Canaan to Haran and as he journeyed he prayed to Abraham's God seeking two things. He requested God's guidance and he prayed for God's steadfast love to be shown to Abraham. What a kind deed and thoughtful prayer from this man who was just a servant to Abraham. Many people do not display such kindness to their employers or to those who have authority over them, especially when they are away from their presence. Abraham's servant was truly and graciously kind.

Rebekah also displayed amazing kindness in her response to Abraham's servant. She did not know who he was or what he had prayed. She did not know that it might lead to her marriage with Isaac. Yet, when the servant asked her if she could provide him with a drink of water, she quickly provided it. Then she went out of her way to water all of the servant's camels as well. Do you have any idea how much water a camel can drink? A thirsty camel can drink as much as 30 gallons of water in about 13 minutes. Wow. This young lady was enthusiastic about her kindness. She wanted to bless the man and his animals until they were all satisfied. Then she offered to bed them down at her father's house for the night.

Taste Test:

Many times people show kindness to those in authority as a way to impress them. It is much rarer to show that kindness without anyone knowing. Jesus taught that when we do 'alms,' that is good deeds of kindness, not to let your left hand know what your right hand is doing. He meant that we should do it privately and not for show. I once knew a young lady who would write secret notes of encouragement to people and slip it under their door. They never knew who gave it.

How can you do a secret act of kindness to someone around you?

- Maybe, without being asked, you could help a family member with a chore.
- Maybe you could write a card to someone, just to encourage him or her.
- Think of ways you can respond to others in kindness as Rebekah did.
- Do you have an elderly neighbor or church member who needs help cleaning around their home? Think it through and help out.

Scraping the Plate:

I Corinthians 13:4 states, *"Love suffers long and is kind..."* Discuss how kindness is a part of love and therefore is displayed the greatest by God Himself. God is love, therefore, He has shown the greatest act of kindness in giving Jesus as our Savior and in the daily acts of kind provision He bestows upon us for life. Let each family member share how he or she see kindness expressed through other family members' love. Discuss ways that those expressions could be better (if necessary) or discuss ways kindness could reach out beyond the family.

Pancakes:

The Holy Spirit enables the work we do. Our competency should be seasoned in kindness as that attracts others to taste and see God's goodness.

HONESTY - the state of being and actions of being good and truthful; free from fraud or deception; not hiding the truth about someone or a situation; not being willing to deceive

"Let not mercy and truth forsake you; bind them around your neck, write them on the tablet of your heart," Proverbs 3:3

Scripture Text: Exodus 18:1-23

The story is told that young George Washington was given a hatchet when he was about six years old. He played with it chopping down his mother's pea-sticks in the garden. When he came upon a tender cherry tree that his father had planted, he tried his ax on its tender frame. Sometime later when his dad came angrily into the house and demanded to know what had happened to the precious cherry tree. Young George declared, "I cannot tell a lie, I cut it with my little hatchet." It is said that George's father kneeled to embrace his son as the anger melted away. He remarked, "My son, that you should not be afraid to tell the truth is more to me than a thousand trees, yes though they were blossomed with silver and had leaves of the purest gold."

Another story remembers how Abraham Lincoln walked several miles to return pennies of change to a customer who had overpaid him. That character gave him the nickname of 'Honest Abe.' Honesty is a characteristic that God required of his leaders in the days of Moses when the Israelites traveled through the wilderness. Moses sat as judge listening to the people's burdens and giving them counsel from God, yet it was a long and wearisome duty. His father-in-law, Jethro, encouraged him to choose men of character who feared God to help. He describes these men as 'men of truth.' It was their responsibility to hear the people's problems would bring to them and judge between them honestly.

Wouldn't it be wonderful if all leaders, judges, and politicians would make honesty their priority? Proverbs 12:22 says, *"Lying lips are an abomination to the Lord, But those who deal truthfully are His delight."* It seems the headlines of newspapers and nightly news on TV are riddled with stories of leaders who have been caught lying.

Amy Rees Anderson of *Forbes* magazine stated that if she could instill one key value into business leaders, it would be that success will come and go, but integrity is forever. Integrity means doing the right things and being honest in all circumstances. Regardless if others are aware, it takes courage to always do the right thing. It also takes a lifetime to build a reputation of honesty, but it can take only a moment to tear it all down.

Many people promise things falsely. Salespeople promise their product will last a lifetime. Politicians promise to balance their spending and save us money. Leaders promise to judge crime fairly and not be influenced by bribery. When we find those leaders who deal honestly, we should delight as God does in them. Dishonest leaders tricked King Darius and had Daniel thrown in the lions' den. They lied that Daniel was a man of poor character because he prayed to God in opposition to the law. This was not true because Daniel was a man of impeccable character who honored his king. When Darius rescued

Daniel from the lions' den the next morning, he cast the dishonest men into the pit with all their families. Daniel, however, was raised to a place of honor where he prospered. God delights in truth and makes people successful when they walk in integrity.

Taste Test:

- Look at ads for products in magazines, on TV, or online. We are told there is supposed to be 'truth in advertising', but sometimes that seems far-fetched.
- Can you find examples of false advertisements?
- Listen to speeches from politicians running for office. Compare their promises to what they actually did while they served. Did they tell the truth?
- Rewrite these ads or speeches into a truthful statement. How could the truth be told to retain a person's integrity?

Scraping the Plate:

Read Proverbs 3:1-10. This passage describes a person of integrity. What are the things that this person does to honor and retain honesty of character? List his/her attributes.

Pancakes:

How we do our work and how we relate to other people in honesty are demonstrations of our faith. We are only as competent as we are honest with the people around us.

HOSPITALITY - being generous and friendly in treatment of visitors; the activity of providing food and refreshment for people who are guests

"Do not withhold good from those to whom it is due when it is your power to do it. Do not say to your neighbor, 'Go, and come again, tomorrow I will give it' when you have it with you."
Proverbs 3:27-28

Scripture Text: Matthew 14:15-21

Hospitality begins in the home. It is crucial that children be taught to share, because it does not come naturally. Psychologists say that the concept of sharing is not fully grasped until a child is 6-8 years old. But as Christians, we believe that character should be modeled and taught from infancy. God is gracious and giving, so we should emulate that character and instill integrity in the next generation. *"They shall teach my people the difference between the holy and the common, and show them how to distinguish between the unclean and the clean,"* Ezekiel 44:23

During the 1970s, my family lived in a small college town. The college's cafeteria was closed on the weekends leaving the students to find meals on their own. Many churches helped by offering a meal on Sunday, but those were sparse and the meals were repetitive. My mom and dad prayed about the opportunity, trusting God to help them be hospitable to meet the students' need. For the next several years our family fed Sunday lunch in our home to as many as 65-70 college students. There were times it exceeded 100. Being hospitable provided opportunity for great times of fellowship and growth. It opened the door for many of these students to connect with our church, develop relationships, and see the hand of the Lord in provision.

My family was lower-middle class. Our home was not what you would call a model home. We lived in an old nursing home building that had been converted into a residence. It was divided into two wings in an 'L' shape. There were lots of bedrooms in the back half, with the kitchen in the middle at the bend. The front of the house was taken up by a family pet store business. Students had to walk through the front to get to the residential part where we all sat and ate. We had plenty of room in the old dining area. There were times, though, when we did not know how God was going to provide the money to buy enough food for meals. Yet He always did. God honored our hospitality and showed Himself capable.

We also offered the spare rooms as places for students to stay when the dorms were closed. We even had one international student from Indonesia who lived with us for one semester. Hospitality was a regular practice as a means of my family's worship and service. I was taught from childhood to give and share what I possessed.

Taste Test:

There are many ways to practice hospitality.

- Bake a batch of cookies or brownies and take them to a neighbor.

- Invite an underprivileged family to your home for dinner.
- Imagine ways that your family could demonstrate hospitality.
- Conceive your plan together and put it into practice.

Scraping the Plate:

Read Acts 21:8-15. Though this story is about Paul on his way to Jerusalem and the danger he faced, one cannot help but notice the hospitality of Philip and his family as they allowed Paul and his company to stay for several days. They cared and prayed for Paul. Share with each other what it might have entailed to have someone stay in your home for several days. What would it cost? How would you have to rearrange people in their rooms to make the guests comfortable? How would it be inconvenient? What would be the blessing that you might receive and do you think it would be worth the inconvenience?

Pancakes:

Hospitality is a service to God. It requires work and love; likewise, we can open our arms and hearts because He did the same for us. God makes us competent to do His service through His grace.

LOYALTY - a feeling of strong support for someone or something

"Nevertheless, I am continually with you; you hold my right hand." Psalm 73:23

Scripture Text: 2 Samuel 15:21-37

Sometimes the greatest act of kindness and love is the loyalty we show by just being beside someone when they are going through a tough time. Sometimes, we don't know all the answers to life's problems or how to fix a situation. In these times, we can help by just being with them. I think that is why we love animals so much. They are always compassionate to be with us when they sense something is wrong. I have seen dogs crawl up on the bed of a sick master and lay close. The dog would whine and cry if it was made to leave.

My brother, Gary, had a pet poodle when we were young. Gary was born with a lung condition that made it difficult to breathe. Many times he ended up in the hospital with lung complications and we did not know if he would live through the night. During the times when he was very ill, his poodle would not leave his side. As long as Gary was at home, that dog followed him everywhere and lay at his feet. When Gary was in the hospital, the poodle lay by the door and cried. The dog would not eat or play or cuddle with anyone else while he was waiting for Gary to return.

King David had loyal friends who stayed beside him and remained true to him in times of difficulty. When David's own son, Absalom, raised a rebellion against his kingdom, David had to flee. David's friend, Ittai, stayed beside him and encouraged him as they fled. Ittai promised to stay with David until death if necessary. David's other friend, Hushai, was a man of great discernment and understanding. David asked him to stay behind in the palace and provide counsel to Absalom, which would contradict the advisors there who were helping Absalom in his rebellion. This required great wisdom and bravery on Hushai's part. Yet, he agreed because he was loyal to David. Being loyal sometimes requires us to stand up against those who oppose the truth and stand beside those we love.

Taste Test:

Being loyal to God means being loyal to those in need and trouble. As we show kindness to the oppressed and hurting, we are demonstrating our loyalty to God. One way to do that is by writing letters of support to missionaries overseas who need encouragement.

- Ask your pastor for the name and address of a missionary, and write expressing your interest for their work and your support to them in prayer.
- Another idea is to write a prisoner who needs encouragement in turning their life over to Christ and staying true to following him. You may be able to get the name of a prisoner by calling a local prison ministry.

Scraping the Plate:

There are various aspects of loyalty: supporting someone in need, staying with someone while he/she is in trouble, or defending someone by standing up for that person. Discuss how you see each of these aspects in the Bible text. Share with young children the necessity of being wise to whom we commit our loyalty. Ahithophel was loyal only to whoever was in power and would benefit him. Why is that not genuine loyalty?

Pancakes:

Loyal employees and faithful workers are a testimony of good integrity. Loyalty can be more valuable to an employer than sheer ability. As Psalm 73:23 states, God is loyal to us.